TROUT FLIES
Naturals
and
Imitations

Trout Flies
Naturals and Imitations

By
CHARLES M. WETZEL

Author of Practical Fly Fishing, The Art of Fly Tying, American Fishing Books

Illustrations by the Author

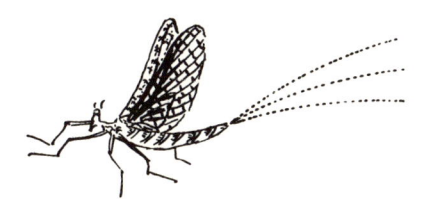

STACKPOLE BOOKS
Harrisburg, Pennsylvania

TROUT FLIES: NATURALS AND IMITATIONS

Copyright © 1955 by Charles M. Wetzel
Copyright © 1979 by The Stackpole Company

Limited facsimile edition, March 1979 $12.00

Published by
STACKPOLE BOOKS
Cameron and Kelker Streets
P.O. Box 1831
Harrisburg, Pa. 17105

Published simultaneously in Don Mills, Ontario, Canada by Thomas Nelson & Sons, Ltd.

All rights reserved, including the right to reproduce this book or portions thereof in any form or by any means, electronic or mechanical, including photocopying, recording, or by any information storage and retrieval system, without permission in writing from the publisher. All inquiries should be addressed to Stackpole Books, Cameron and Kelker Streets, P.O. Box 1831, Harrisburg, Pennsylvania 17105.

Library of Congress Catalog Card No. 55-11692
ISBN 0-8117-1739-3

Printed in the U.S.A.

To my ten-year-old son

Bill

who likes to fish with a fly.

Contents

	Page
Chapter I Fancy and Natural Flies	1
Chapter II General Introduction to Stream Entomology	5
Chapter III Nymphs	15
Chapter IV Collecting Stream Insects	25
Chapter V Scientific Stream Entomology	29
Chapter VI The Catalog	47
Chapter VII Emergence Tables	87
Chapter VIII Imitating the Natural Insect	93
Chapter IX Transplanting Stream Insects	105
Chapter X The Gordon Quill Fly	117
Chapter XI Fishing the Wet Fly	123
Chapter XII Fishing the Dry Fly	129
Chapter XIII Fishing the Nymph	133
Chapter XIV Pages from the Diary	137
Chapter XV Fisherman's Weather	149
Appendix Reference Literature	152

CHAPTER I

Fancy or Natural Flies

THE OTHER evening, while going over my angling library, I chanced to open up that bulky volume, *Favorite Flies,* by Mary Orvis Marbury. While I idly turned the pages, one or two paragraphs in the book claimed my attention, not only because they were so prophetic, but also because the author so clearly and acutely sensed that the old time trout flies were on the way out, and that a new era or cycle in fly fishing was developing. Allow me to quote the paragraph.

"As streams have become depleted and fish more shy they need to be fished with greater caution and skill, and there is therefore a greater demand for smaller flies delicately tied in colors less gaudy than those needed for the flies used in wild unfrequented rivers and lakes."

How prophetic was the above! Now that some fifty years have elapsed since these words were written, suppose we sift the ashes in search of the pure gold, insofar as it relates to the present day.

Gone are those wild, unfrequented rivers and lakes, and gone with them too are those gaudy trout flies so beautifully and artistically lithographed in *Favorite Flies.* In fairness it must be said that these gaudy creations were the aftermath of that wild orgy, when it was discovered that bass would rise to and take a fly, provided that it reflected all the colors of the rainbow. If such flies were good for bass, then they should also prove attractive to trout, it was reasoned. And it must be confessed that in a limited way the above proved true, so long as angling was confined to wild, uneducated fish. Disciples of this gaudy creation cult included nearly all the old time anglers of the eighties and nineties, such as Seth Green, Reuben Wood, Fred Mather, Charles Orvis, A. N. Cheney, W. C. Prime, J. L. King, C. W. Stevens, Kit Clark, T. S. Updegraff, Ned Buntline, W. David Tomlin, J. A. Henshall, George Dawson, Charles Hallock, Henry Wells, W. C. Harris, F. J. Fitch, W. Thompson, J. G. Rich, T. S. Morrell, D. W. Cross, and a host of others. A few of them had the temerity to state that the most successful trout flies were those patterned after natural insects, but popular opinion, backed by the most expert fishermen of the day, decreed otherwise with the consequence that such remarks or observations were given little weight or credence.

However, as I have mentioned, a new era or cycle in the history of fly fishing was developing. The brook trout were rapidly diminishing in number due to the inroads of civilization, and these fish were being replaced by the brown trout, a moody, wary, and discriminating feeder on natural insects. No longer could every Tom, Dick, and Harry equipped with a cast of three wet flies such as the Red Ibis, Parmacheenee Belle, and Silver Doctor, venture out and return with a creelful of trout as in "the good old days." It just simply couldn't be done! What was needed to catch these fish were flies more sober in appearance and more nearly approximating the fly on the water.

And now we come to that second paragraph in *Favorite Flies* that struck my interest. Again allow me to quote it.

"At present, fishermen are chiefly indebted to the fly makers of Great Britain for copies of the insects alluring to game fish. Their experience extends back for centuries before our time or country even, and until we have studied more thoroughly our own stream life, we do well to abide by many of their conclusions; but there can be no question that in the years to come the differences between the insects of the two countries will be better understood and defined, and that a collection of water insects interesting to the fishermen of America with directions for accurate imitations, arranged after the manner of Alfred Ronald's *Fly Fishers Entomology* would be of value."

As prophesied by Mrs. Marbury, a number of works relating to trout stream insects—insofar as they concern the American fly fisher—have appeared in this half-century interval. In sequence these are: *American Trout Stream Insects,* by Louis Rhead; *A Book of Trout Flies,* by Preston Jennings; *Practical Fly Fishing,* by the author of this work; Art Flick's *Streamside Guide;* and Bus Grove's *The Lure and Lore of Trout Fishing.* It must be confessed that none of these books had a tremendous sale—few fishing books have. After more than one decade only *Practical Fly Fishing* is almost exhausted, which gives one a fair indication of what the thinking angler desires.

And now suppose we look at some of the flies which have proven their worth on our highly educated trout of today. No longer will the modern fly book contain such old timers as the Parmacheenee Belle, etc.; but throughout, there will be noticed an absence of gaiety and gaudiness. These modern flies are imitations of insects that can be noticed flying over the trout streams. Among them, imitating the stone fly group, will be found the Yellow Sally, Willow, and the Light, Green, and Black Stone flies; those imitating May flies are the Green, Black, Grey, and Yellow Drakes, the Pale Evening Dun and

Fancy and Natural Flies

Spinner, the Red, Black, Brown, and Ginger Quills, the March Brown, the Great Red Spinner, the Iron Blue Dun, the Jenny Spinner, the Golden Spinner, and the White Gloved Howdy; those imitating caddis flies are the Spotted Sedge, the Grannom, the Brown Silverhorns and the White, Green, and Black Caddis imitations; the crane fly group is represented by the Yellow and Ginger Spider; while among the miscellaneous will be found the Fish Fly, the Alder, and the Black and Green Midges. Nymphs imitating all the above groups are also represented. Outside of the above no fancy flies will be noted, excepting of course, streamers, bucktails, marabous, feather minnows, and the like, which can hardly be classed as true trout flies. The latter, with all their gaudiness, will take trout, and larger ones too, but such lures are perhaps taken for some of our highly colored minnows or young brook trout.

Suppose we look a little more closely at some of these imitations of natural insects. In general they do not deviate much from the old time gaudy flies, except possibly in the absence of high colors.

An exception to the above are the imitations of the crane fly group. You will notice that extra long spade or saddle hackles are used. Some time ago, over at the Anglers' Club in New York, Edward R. Hewitt was telling me about the success he was having with large spiders or lightly dressed, long hackled flies, which when skipped and pulled over the water caused trout to go crazy. I told him that I observed the same effect with the long legged crane fly imitations, and he attributed the success of these flies to the light spots set up when the hackle pierced the surface film of the water. Hewitt has christened his long hackled flies the "Neversink Skaters," and after fishing his water I had an opportunity to see their effectiveness. Trout leaped above the surface after the flies, one after another, and all in all, it was quite a display.

Among the May fly imitations you will observe both duns and spinners, as well as both male and female in certain species. It will be remembered that the dun represents the insect immediately after it has cast the nymphal skin. At this time it presents a very dull appearance due to the loosening of the sub imago skin that it will shortly shed to become a spinner. The spinner is usually differently colored from the dun in both wings and body.

Then again there will be imitations that do not represent any specific fly, but are tied up to bring out the most striking features of the genus taken collectively. I would say that the Quill Gordon is of this variety, although this may be open to question. Some of the imitations of the female spinners have an enlarged bulb near the bend of the hook, which is supposed to represent the eggsack of its prototype; examples of these are the Pale Evening Spinner and the Brown Quill Spinner. Some of these spinners also have upright wings, while others have them extended in a horizontal plane, the latter position imitating the spent fly as it floats downstream in its death throes, never to fly again. This spent position is common to both the male and the female, but the female imitation will probably prove the most successful, since she dies on the water more frequently than the male.

The stone flies, caddis flies, fish flies, etc. call for no special comment, but it will be observed that the nymphs differ from the usual market run in that they bear a striking resemblance to the naturals found on and around the stream bed.

Here in our heavily fished Eastern trout streams, we have found through experience that it pays rich dividends to match the fly on the water. Some doubters claim that they can catch just as many trout on a highly colored, fancy, dry fly as they could by using a close imitation; but after one or two trials, such would-be iconoclasts invariably admit their error. Color and form are far more important than some anglers realize. I believe in all sincerity that if a questionnaire were distributed to all the fly fishers in the East, nine out of ten would reply that the fly should conform to the insect on the water.

And what has brought about this transition? Simply this: the old time flies no longer produce, and fishermen realized that if they wanted to catch trout which were daily becoming more educated, they must give them something which is more than a mere bunch of gaudily colored feathers.

CHAPTER II

General Introduction to Stream Entomology

THE WRITER spent considerable time, a number of years ago, on Eastern waters, studying the trout stream insects, particularly those that concerned the fly fisher. The results of these studies were originally published in the magazine, The *Pennsylvania Angler* and afterwards in the book, *Practical Fly Fishing,* and the response to the study was highly gratifying.

Approximately 60 common trout stream insects were identified, described, and drawn to scale; and for the benefit of the fly-tyer, practical information was included for the dressings of their imitations.

Perhaps it might be well to say a few words concerning the evolution of the study. Briefly, the primary purpose was to secure specimens so that I could use them as models when tying up my artificial flies. For three years, throughout the trout fishing seasons, the writer was almost daily on the trout streams, collecting, observing, and recording. Practically all the larger streams in Pennsylvania furnished specimens, particularly Penns Creek, Pine Creek, Brodheads Creek, the Loyalsock, and many others. Some 300 flies comprised the collection; however, the list was narrowed down to 60 since it was felt desirable to list only those insects which (a) were common and had a wide distribution and (b) those on which trout actively feed.

A record was also kept as to when the insects were over the water, information which led to the compiling of an Emergence Table. It was felt that the recording of this information could not help but be valuable, for if the trout were rising well to a certain hatch of flies on a certain day, the chances were that a repetition of the same thing would occur in following years, perhaps not always on the same day, but very close to it. With this information on hand and with artificials closely resembling the natural insect, one could then gauge the time of arrival on a certain stream and

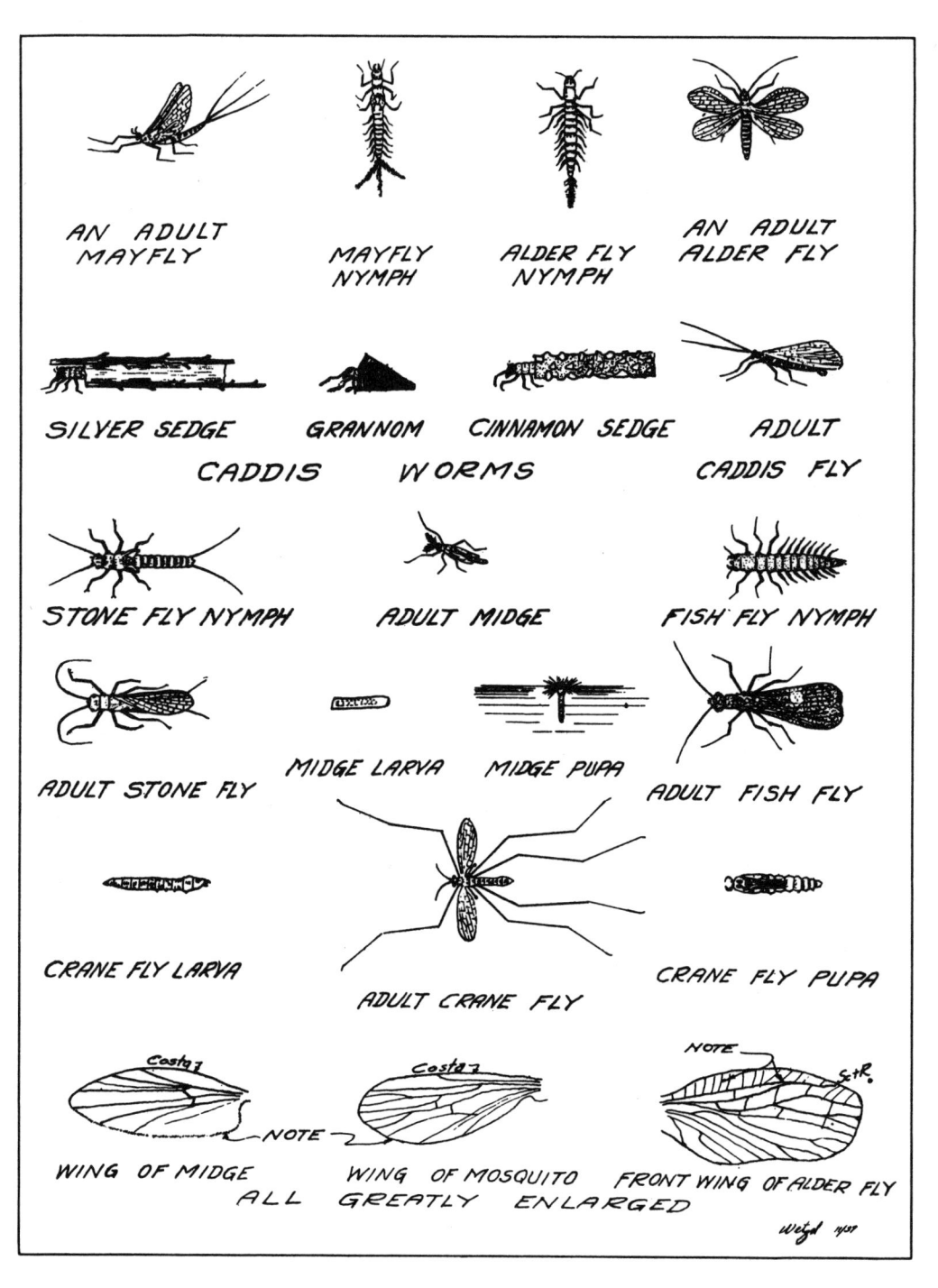

PLATE I.

General Introduction to Stream Entomology

at the same time be reasonably confident as to the flies which would be over the water. And the Emergence Table has proven its worth! One of the most startling things brought out in the study and confirmed during later years, was the regularity with which the flies year after year appeared, invariably within a few calendar days of each other.

The cataloguing of the flies represented a great amount of work. Many of the Mayflies were identified by the writer, but all those hereinafter described were checked and rechecked by specialists in the various groups so as to avoid any possibility of error. Those who have checked identification for me include McDonnough, Ross, Needham, Alexander, Betten, and a great many others.

Now that some 15 years have passed, with interest in the study still running high, it was thought desirable to revise and republish the entomology, bringing it up to date and in line with present day knowledge. It was also thought desirable to include information on how to collect, preserve, and identify trout stream insects, thereby making it a complete fly fishers' entomology. Perhaps the information contained will prove an incentive and spur others on to continue this pioneer work—the first of its kind to be published in America.

IDENTIFICATION OF TROUT STREAM INSECTS

A great many anglers are of the opinion that a cursory glance is all that is needed to identify those insects commonly found over the trout streams. This is true insofar as the order is concerned, but to determine the insect as to family, genus, and species is quite another matter. Later on we will attempt to show the method of procedure in tracking down the specific name of an insect, but for the time being, suppose we content ourselves in becoming familiar with the orders of the various groups most commonly encountered. Refer to the sketch, which will give one an idea of their general appearance.

MAYFLIES

These insects are the favorites of all fly fishermen, and more trout flies have been patterned after them than all the other groups combined. They are among the earliest of our flies that hover over the water, and at various times they appear in such numbers that the bushes bordering the streams are bent down under their weight.

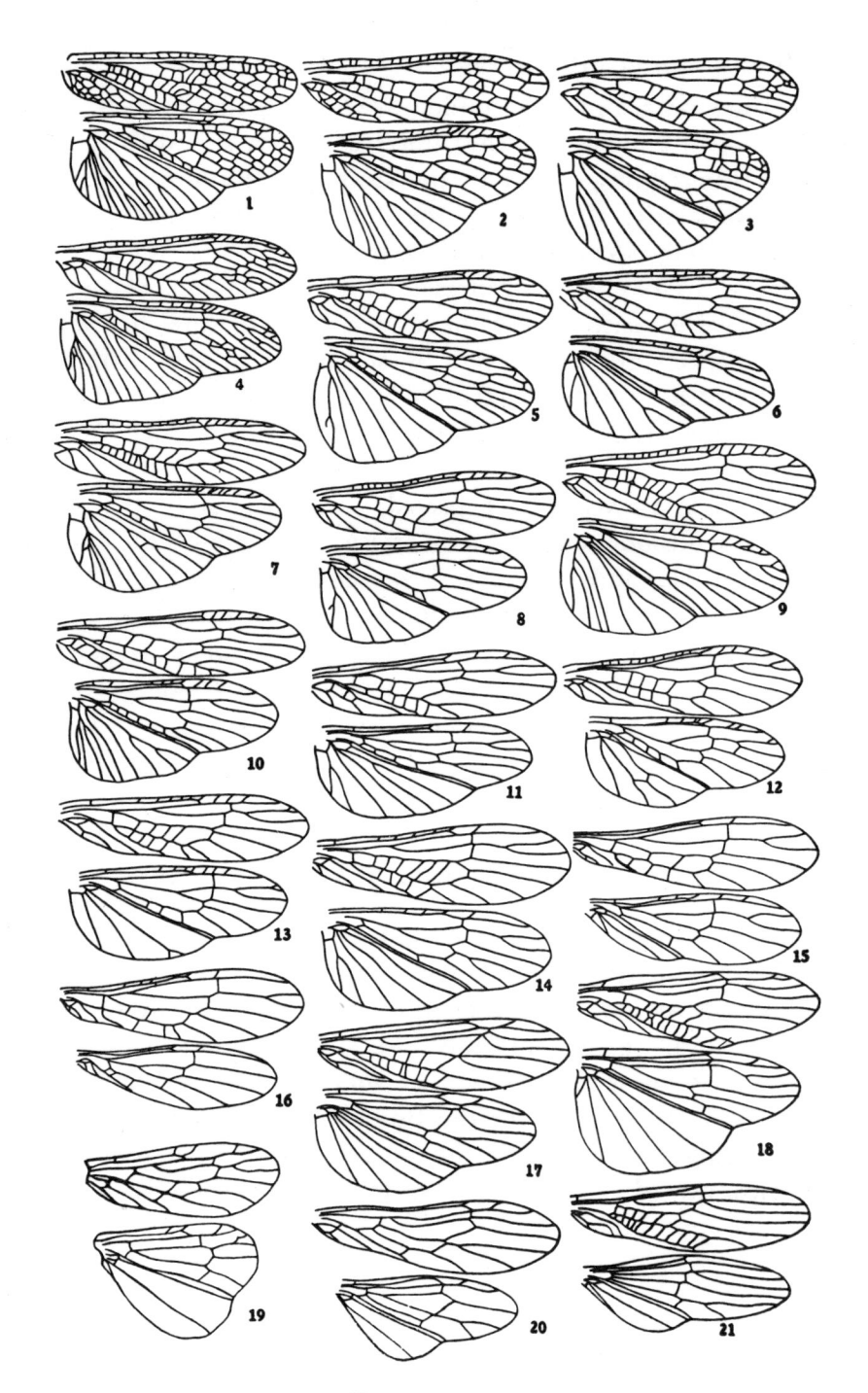

PLATE II. WINGS OF STONE FLIES.

1. Pteronarcys 2. Pteronarcella 3. Periodes 4. Acroneuria 5. Isogenus
6. Kathroperla 7. Perla 8. Perlesta 9. Peltoperla 10. Perlinella
11. Atoperla 12. Neoperla 13. Paraperla 14. Isoperla 15. Alloperla
16. Chloroperla 17. Nemoura 18. Taeniopteryx 19. Capnella 20. Capnia
21. Leuctra

General Introduction to Stream Entomology

The adults are fragile insects; they are equipped with two or three long tails and usually two pairs of wings, the hind pair much smaller than those in front. They range in size from little *Caenis*, whose wings are less than one-eighth of an inch long to the big May fly *Ephemera guttulata*, whose wings are about an inch in length. Adult May flies do not walk, run, nor climb, and can usually be seen sitting quietly on the brush at the water's edge. In repose the body is curved upwards, the wings are held vertically, and the long fore feet are extended forward like a pair of antennae.

Mayflies are peculiar in that they moult after they assume the winged stage. Transformation from nymph to the winged state occurs at the top of water—the castoff nymphal skin floats away—and the insect, rather weak in its flight, makes its way to the nearby bushes and trees. It is now known among fishermen as a dun (entomologists call it a sub imago) and it is clothed with a fine skin, which is shed after a resting period varying from a couple of hours to a couple of days. After casting off this skin they appear in brighter colors and are then known among anglers as spinners (the imago stage of the entomologist).

The adult males dance up and down, fly in companies, and the females come out to meet them in the air. When the mating flight is over, they fall exhausted on the water with wings outstretched, and in this phase they are known among fishermen as *spent spinners, spent wings,* or *spent flies*.

In the nymphal or immature stage the Mayfly generally has three tails, and may be recognized by the single tarsal claws and the gills on the side of the abdomen. They live entirely in the water, and are found under stones and in a variety of places on the stream bed. (See Chapter 3 entitled "Trout Stream Nymphs.")

Caddis Flies

The larvae of these insects, known as caddis worms or caddis creepers, are encased in tubes or sheaths which they drag along over the stream bed. These cases or homes in which they dwell are constructed out of a variety of materials, such as sand, stones, leaves, bark, shells, twigs, etc., and vary from one-fourth of an inch to over two inches in length. Each family prefers a type of architecture distinctly its own, and the shapes are many and varied. (See sketch of Caddis cases in Chapter III entitled "Trout Stream Nymphs.")

When ready to assume the pupa stage, the larva fastens its case to some support and closes up the opening with a thick silk mesh. After the body has altered its shape and the wings have formed, the pupa, enclosed in a thin skin, tears open the silk screen door at the mouth of the case and rises to the surface. The covering skin then splits open, and the fly emerges and grasps some object upon which it can climb above the water to dry its wings.

Adult caddis flies have long, thread-like antennae, which usually project straight out in front; the hind wings are shorter and broader than the fore wings, and both pairs rest slanting like a roof over the abdomen when the insect is resting. In general, they are hairy, moth-like insects, delicately colored, and appear in greatest numbers at dusk or after nightfall. Some caddis flies are of particular importance to the wet fly fishermen due to the female's habit of swimming and crawling beneath the water to lay her eggs.

STONE FLIES

The nymph of the stone fly prefers those stretches of a stream where the water flows swiftly over a rocky bottom. As their name implies, these insects make their homes under stones on the stream bed, but the Willow is sometimes found in the leaf drifts. The nymph may be recognized by its two tails, the fine gills under the thorax, and by the possession of the two tarsal claws.

About the first of May, or earlier, when ready to change into flies, they fasten themselves to stones at the water's edge, and there the nymphal skin splits open, permitting the fly to escape. Certain types also clamber above the water on projecting sticks or weeds to transform. Different species emerge at various times of the year. Among the four main families the *Capniidae* or small black forms appear earliest, often while the snow is still on the ground; the dark, blackest winged *Nemouridae* next follow in early spring; the big *Pteronarcidae* come next; and the green and yellow forms fill out the season.

The adult flies are heavy in flight and are easily captured. A favorite resting place of theirs is on the underside of leaves. Last season on Young Womans Creek, I secured quite a few specimens of the stone fly *Perla* simply by shaking the bushes along the stream and picking the fallen flies off the ground. The distinguishing features of the adults are the wide, notched, and pleated hind wings (see illustration entitled Wings of Stoneflies); the two tarsal claws; the broad flat head; and the manner in which the wings rest flat over the abdomen.

Stone flies rarely appear in the immense swarms characterized by the Mayflies and caddis flies, yet they are of the utmost importance to the fly fisher. With the exception of the green and yellow stone flies, the majority of these insects are of subdued colors, brown predominating.

CRANE FLIES

These flies appear in the greatest numbers during the late summer, but are quite common throughout the trout fishing season. The larvae,

General Introduction to Stream Entomology

commonly known as water worms, are found in the hollow stems of submerged twigs and in the muck and leaf drifts of streams. Some are also found under stones and in the sand on the stream bed. Some of the larva are quite small, while others attain two inches or more in length. Due to its long legs, the adult fly can hardly be mistaken for any other insect. In the rear of the wings are a pair of knobbed halters, which will further serve as a means of identification.

MIDGES

These small insects appear later in the season, and usually at a time when trout refuse all but the smallest flies. They frequently appear in immense swarms, and at such times their pupa cases can often be noticed in thick, scum-like patches on the top of the water. Doubtless the majority of fly fishermen have witnessed large swarms of these flies and believed them to be mosquitoes, for they resemble them very much—only they do not bite.

The larva, worm-like in form, live in thin, filmy tubes attached to stones and leaves underwater, sometimes at a great depth. There are two principal varieties, the white and the red. Both are found on our streams, but the latter prefer lake regions, where they are known as Blood Worms.

When ready to change into flies, the pupa rises to the top of the water and floats there in a vertical position, descending when disturbed but quickly rising again. Their most conspicuous feature in this stage is the tube gills, which resemble small silvery brushes.

The adults are slender and gnat-like in form, and the male fly is conspicuous by the large, fan shaped, feathery antennae. The midges may be distinguished from mosquitoes by the rear part of the wing (see sketch).

MISCELLANEOUS FLIES

Under this heading appears those flies found in and around the water, such as the Fish Fly, the Alder, the Scud, and the Red Legged March Fly, as well as those land flies that drop or jump on the water or are blown on the water by winds, such as the Blue Bottle, the House Fly, the Golden Eyed Gauze Wing, the Deer Fly, the Ants, Grasshoppers, and the Japanese Beetle.

FISH FLIES—These flies are quite common on our trout streams but never appear in the great swarms characterized by the Mayflies and caddis flies. *Chauliodes lunatus*, the most common species, has color. Its brownish black wings are traversed by a broad white band, and in addition there appear numerous small whitish patches and spots.

The fish fly and the smaller alder fly both belong to the order *Megaloptera*, and the wings are the distinguishing peculiarities of this group. In addition to the numerous traverse veins in the costal area, the sub costa and first radius veins are apically fused. (See sketch, which is typical for both the fish fly and the alder.)

The larvae of the fish fly resemble hellgrammites and are about one-half their length. They live entirely in the water and are commonly found in the mud, on the underside of submerged timbers, and under stones on the stream bed.

ALDER FLIES—This insect, known as *Sialis infumata*, is the prototype of that familiar trout fly known as the Alder. Like the fish fly, it is quite commonly found on our trout streams. but never appears in great swarms.

The adult insect is considerably smaller than the fish fly, and has a wingspread of approximately one inch. It has black legs and antennae, smoky black wings, and a black body. The nymph, conspicuous by its single hairy tail, may be found buried in the sand and gravel, sometimes a foot below the bed of the stream.

SCUD—The Scuds, or Fresh Water Shrimp appears in almost unbelievable numbers, especially in swampy streams where watercress abounds. Apparently they feed on the roots, for they congregate there by the hundreds. They are almost invariably found in copula, and appear to have difficulty in finding a sufficient change of mates. *Gammarus minus,* a common species, has a transparent amber colored body about one-half an inch long and has bright, black eyes. The legs are composed of fourteen pairs, eight on the thorax and six on the abdomen, those on the thorax being the longest.

RED LEGGED MARCH FLY—When once seen, this insect cannot be forgotten, for its legs are a combination of brilliant blood red and jet black, the red part being on the thickest part of the leg, that is, the femur. It is a true fly, having only one pair of wings, about three-eighths of an inch long, which are light black in color. The pupa stage of the insect is black clothed with whitish hair along the sides. The pupa stage of the insect is found buried in the bank of the stream, approximately at the water's edge or slightly above it. After transforming to the winged stage, the fly staggers forth from its burrow and falls into the water, where it can be quite often noticed struggling on the surface.

BLUE BOTTLE, MOUSE FLY, GOLDEN EYED GAUZE WING, DEER FLY, ANT, JAPANESE BEETLE, AND GRASSHOPPER—These insects are so well known that I feel it unnecessary to add anything further concerning them. They are chiefly taken by trout when blown on the water by strong winds. Charlie Fox and the Harrisburg Fly Fishers are all strong advocates of terrestrial flies. Through the years they have been imitating these insects, changing this and changing that, and through constant experimentation they have finally evolved artificials that cannot be beaten on the limestone streams of central Pennsylvania. They attach great significance to the little Leafhoppers (Jassids), the winged Red and Black Ants, the Jap Beetle and Grasshoppers, all of which find their way to the waters of the meadow streams which these men fish regularly.

CHAPTER III

Nymphs

MOST OF US, I think, have experienced the time when the air was crowded with Mayflies, the trout were rising furiously with here and there a tail fin showing above the water, and yet regardless of what dry fly we tied on, all our efforts in our attempt to catch them proved futile. Such a situation taxes one's patience to the utmost, for everyone likes to catch fish, or at least have rises. We try to console ourselves with the thought that our artificial, although a fair imitation, is only one fly among the thousands that are on the water, and the trout haven't found it. But is that the case?

Frankly it is not. The trout acting in the manner described above are feeding on nymphs which are floating near the surface—so near the top that one naturally believes from the character of the rise that the trout are taking the winged fly. It is difficult at times to distinguish whether the trout are taking nymphs or winged flies. One of the surest indications, though not an infallible one, can be judged from the rise.

Whenever a bulge appears on the water, followed by a glimpse of a tail fin above the surface—as if the trout was standing on its head—the trout is taking nymphs. At such times the trout takes up a position near the top of the water, and as the nymphs—usually in flushes—rise to the surface to effect their metamorphosis to the winged stage, they are caught in the ascent. This position is also assumed by the trout as they root around in the stream bed in shallow water trying to dislodge nymphs and other larva from the stones. Another good indication that trout are taking nymphs can be obtained from the streaks that follow in the wake of fish, as they swirl about feeding avidly on the floating pupae which are poised just under the surface waiting for the nymphal skin to split open. This is particularly noticeable on the quiet placid pools and is at times a scene of great activity, for the trout feed ravenously on the practically quiescent nymph, as if knowing the winged fly will soon emerge and fly away.

So much has been written about nymph fishing during recent years that I hesitate to add more to the subject. Yet when one carefully digests such articles, a great number advocate fishing the nymph in a manner that is totally unlike the movements of the natural prototype.

I have been fishing nymphs for a great many years and have caught considerable trout on them too, but frankly, this type of fishing does not appeal to me nearly so much as fishing wet or dry fly. Undoubtedly however, a fertile field is open to the angling fraternity and considerable originality can be exercised by the fishermen who tie their own flies, for without a question of doubt, nymphs comprise the trout's principal diet. I have a habit of making a post mortem examination of the stomach contents of all trout I kill, and numerous autopsies bear out the above statement. In addition to the usual conglomeration of flies, snails, beetles, shrimps, etc., one can always find nymphs—sometimes still alive and wiggling. Knowing then that they comprise the trout's principal diet, it behooves one to learn their habits so that the artificial can be fished realistically. To simplify matters all underwater insects in the following pages will be called nymphs, regardless of whether they are in the larvae or pupae stages.

Mayfly Nymphs

These insects are probably dominant on the stream beds on the majority of our trout streams. Like trout, they always lie with their heads upstream, waiting for food to be carried down to them by the current. They are of the utmost importance to the nymph fisher, and as such it might be well to review some of the facts elsewhere written concerning them. We will remember that the fly in the winged state exists in two stages, that is, the sub-imago and the imago. The flies in these two stages are commonly known among fishermen as *duns* and *spinners;* the large flies are also known as drakes, and within nomenclature no distinction is made as to whether they are in the sub-imago or imago stages.

The eggs, after being deposited by the spinner or imago, sink to the bottom and shortly hatch into nymphs. During this period of growth the insect moults many times; and immediately after each moult, the body expands in size and changes its form, always progressing towards the winged insect. These instars, or periods between successive moults—in which no visible body changes occur—are said to number as high as twenty.

Slow and fast moving waters are each peculiar in having types of nymphs distinctly their own.

Nymphs

SWIFT WATER MAYFLY NYMPHS

These are of three different kinds: (A) those under stones, (B) those ranging freely about on the stream bed and on crests of dams, wiers, etc., and (C) those sprawling in the leaf drifts and in the muck in eddies.

(A) *Nymphs found under stones* are usually flat shaped. Examples of winged flies transforming from this group are the Red Quill, Ginger Quill, March Brown, and White Mayfly (see the Catalogue for a pictorial representation; see especially the Ginger Quill and Red Quill nymphs, which are typical for those found under stones). These nymphs are lovers of dark places. When one lifts up a stone on a stream bed, they may be seen quickly scrambling towards the underside, away from the light. Many people believe that trout only prey on them when they rise to transform into winged flies, but such is not the case. On dark cloudy days and at night they come out from under the stones and wander freely about. This is the time when fly fishing is best, due entirely to underwater activity, which really starts moving. To substantiate the above statement, time after time I have taken trout whose stomachs contained deeply buried nymphs that were weeks away from the time when they would transform into winged flies. Conversely, it is true that trout are much like hogs, always rooting around and overturning small stones in their search for nymphs; however, I am sure that the great majority are captured on dark, cloudy days at which time they wander about freely on the stream bed.

(B) *The nymphs that range freely about on the stream bed* are streamlined and offer little resistance to the water rushing past them. While at rest, they may be noticed hanging on by their feet, their bodies swaying with the current. They skip about from place to place, but are not such active swimmers as the free ranging type found in slower moving waters. Examples of winged flies transforming from this group are the Iron Blue Dun, Jenny Spinner, and White Gloved Howdy (see the Catalogue for a pictorial representation; see especially the Iron Blue Dun Nymph, which is typical for the group).

(C) *The nymphs found among the leaf drifts and in the muck on the stream bed* are of two varieties, one a spiny, stiff legged type, and the other, a flatter, smoother nymph that lives on the bottom amid rather clean dirt, silt, and sand. An example of a winged fly transforming from the latter type is the Golden Spinner (see the Catalogue for a pictorial representation; see especially the Golden Spinner Nymph, which is typical for the type).

Slow Water Mayfly Nymphs

These are of three different kinds: (D) those that burrow in the mud, sand, and gravel, (E) those that climb among the weeds or dart about on the stream bed, and (F) those that sprawl upon the bottom.

(D) *The nymphs that burrow in the mud, sand, and gravel* are peculiar in having long horn-like mandibles, which are used for lifting the roof of its burrow; these, in conjunction with its strong front feet, are its principal means of digging in. Years ago, when I endeavored to transplant the nymphs of *Ephemera guttulata* from Penns Creek to Middle Creek, I found many of them at a foot or more below the stream bed; yet throughout the season, I have taken trout whose stomachs contained these nymphs. In general, most of the digging nymphs are light colored. Examples of winged flies transforming from this group are the Green, Black, Grey, Brown, Yellow, and Dark Green Drakes (see the Catalogue for a pictorial representation of the above; see especially the Green Drake Nymph, which is typical for the group).

(E) *The nymphs that climb among the weeds or that dart about on the stream bed* are conspicuous by their heavily fringed tails, which serve as a strong tail fin. They are very agile, darting here and there with the swiftness and sureness of a young pickerel. In this respect they are assisted by their powerful gill plates on the sides, which help them in jumping. Examples of winged flies transforming from this group are the Black and Brown Quills (see the Catalogue for their pictures; see especially the Brown Quill Nymph, which is typical for the group).

(F) *The nymphs that sprawl upon the bottom* are hairy, frowsy looking forms, with stout bodies and thinly fringed tails. Silt adheres to the hair on their bodies, giving excellent concealment. Scraped up with the silt on the stream bed, one seldom notices them until they start moving. They move about very little, their safety lying in escaping observation rather than in flight. Some, like *Ephemerella fuscata,* have conspicuous, large gill plates on the sides. An example of a winged fly transforming from this group is the Pale Evening Dun (see the Catalogue for a pictorial representation; see especially the Olive Dun Nymph, which is typical for the group).

Stone Fly Nymphs

Underneath the rocks, on the beds of swift flowing streams, live the stone fly nymphs. They bear a striking resemblance to some of the mayfly nymphs earlier described; however, they can be identified and separated from them by the presence of long antennae, fine hairy gills under the thorax, and the two claws on the feet. They are not only dwellers under stones but may also be found under drifted leaves, debris, etc. Needham mentions that at least one year seems to be required to complete the life cycle, and in some of the larger species two or three years may be consumed. The nymph is said to complete as high as twenty instars before transforming into the winged insect.

When ready to change into flies they fasten themselves by a glue-like substance to the underside of stones at the water's edge, and there the nymphal skin splits open, permitting the fly to escape. When this occurs the rocks along the stream can often be noticed strewn with nymphal skins, curiously like the living nymphs in shape, but dry and empty and with a gaping slit along the back of the thorax, through which the fly escaped.

Caddis Worms

The stomach contents of trout usually reveal a quantity of small stones, sticks, sand, etc. These are the undigested remains of caddis cases which the trout ate to get the worm which lived within. These cases can often be noticed on the stream bed and their shapes are many and varied (see sketch illustrating various types of architecture).

Caddis flies usually lay their eggs upon the water or descend beneath the surface and attach them to stones with a jelly-like substance. I have had them deposit their eggs upon my waders underneath the surface, and the eggs were most difficult to remove. The larva, when hatched out, at once starts making the case in which it spends the larval stage. These cases are sometimes constructed out of sticks and bark; then again, they may be composed entirely of sand, stone, and pieces of gravel. These they cause to adhere by means of a glue-like thread until they have formed about themselves a case; the outside covering shows the substance of which it is composed, while the interior of the structure is perfectly smooth and round and lined with a thin coating of the glutinous substance that assisted in its construction.

While abiding in these cases or sheaths they are known as caddis worms, caddis creepers, stick worms, etc. The cases vary in length from less than a half inch to over two inches, and their diameter (stone cases) is about three-eighths of an inch. The larva by thrusting forth from its case its head and forefeet, drags the case along wherever it desires to go. It is usually found in the quiet, shallow water, and the portable house is one of nature's safeguards to protect it from larger predatory insects and fish. This is no barrier, however, to trout who eat cases and all.

20 *Trout Flies—Naturals and Imitations*

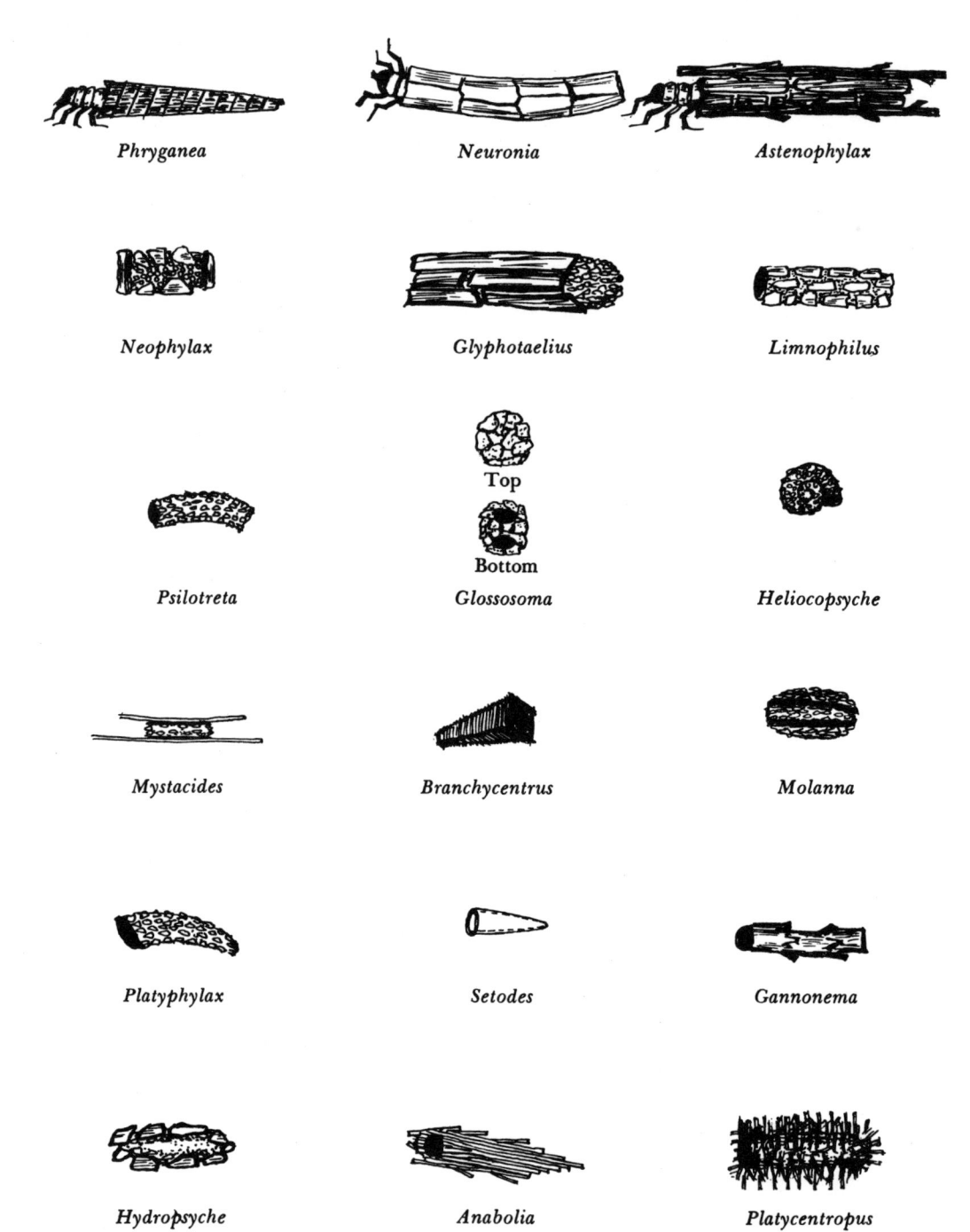

Phryganea *Neuronia* *Astenophylax*

Neophylax *Glyphotaelius* *Limnophilus*

Top
Bottom
Psilotreta *Glossosoma* *Heliocopsyche*

Mystacides *Branchycentrus* *Molanna*

Platyphylax *Setodes* *Gannonema*

Hydropsyche *Anabolia* *Platycentropus*

PLATE III. CADDIS CASES.

Nymphs

The lower end of the case is practically closed, having only a small air hole. It is very difficult to pull the worm from its case without tearing it in two, for at the hind end of the body is a pair of horny hooks which take firm hold on the inside of the case. To remove it without violence it is best to split the sheath.

When ready to assume the pupa form, the larva closes up the opening of the case with a thick silk mesh. While so enclosed, the insect undergoes a change peculiar to the pupa; the wings form and the body alters its shape. After a time the fully formed pupa, which is enveloped in a thin skin, tears open the silken screen door at the mouth of the case and rises to the surface. The thin skin then splits open and the fully developed fly emerges and grasps some object upon which it can climb above the water to expand and dry its wings.

CRANE FLY LARVA

Adult crane flies usually lay their eggs in the habitat frequented by the larva. This is accomplished by rising and falling dipping down into the water surface, a number of eggs being deposited at each descent. A short time later the female dies; in fact, the adult's life lasts about two weeks at the most.

The larval stage is spent both on land and in water. Those that frequent the water are known among anglers as water worms, and they are found in a variety of places, such as in the leaf drifts, the stems of waterlogged twigs, under stones, and in the muck and sand of the stream bed. *Antocha saxicola,* the Yellow Spider, is strictly aquatic and passes both larval and pupal stages in a silken net attached to stones on the stream bed. These nets are covered with fine pebbles and vegetable matter and usually bridge longitudinally some crevice in the rock. *Tipula bella* and *T. bicornis,* the Whirling Crane fly and the Orange Crane fly, spend the larval stage in the water but pupate on the land. The length of the larval stage varies from a month to almost a year in some species.

MISCELLANEOUS NYMPHS AND LARVAE

Under this heading, brief mention will be made of Dragon and Damsel Fly nymphs, and Dobson Fly, Midge, Alder, and Fish Fly larvae.

DRAGON AND DAMSEL FLY NYMPHS

Dragon and Damsel Fly nymphs are found on the larger streams and furnish an abundant food supply for trout. Except for the common Little Damsel Fly nymph, *Ischnura verticalis,* the majority are too large for successful imitation. Some are found in the muck of the stream bed, while others live among the weeds that grow in the water.

The nymph of the Damsel Fly may be recognized by its long cylindrical body and the three leaf-like tails, which are in reality gills. Dragon Fly nymphs have stout bodies and are found in a variety of forms. They have no external gills as in the Damsel Flies, but have three triangular spine-like processes at the end of the abdomen. The nymph may also be identified by its prominent labium, or lower lip, which flap-like, covers its face like a mask.

Both Dragon and Damsel Fly nymphs emerge from the water by climbing up the stems of aquatic plants. Transformation to the winged fly occurs some distance above the water, and the cast off nymphal skins clinging to the willows are a familiar sight.

Dobson Fly, Alder, and Fish Fly Larva

The larva of the Dobson Fly, *Corydalis cornuta,* is the well-known Hellgrammite found under stones in the swift, shallow riffles. Hellgrammites are black in color and when full grown attain a length of around three inches, much too large for successful imitation. Trout feed on them, however, and they furnish an abundant food supply. Around June the Hellgrammite leaves the ground and pupates under stones on the bank of the stream. In this stage it is white in color and transformation to the winged fly quickly follows. The adults are nocturnal in habits, and the fluttering noise they make while flying over the water is familiar to all anglers.

The larva of the Alder Fly, *Sialis infumata,* burrows in the sand and gravel on the stream bed, sometimes a foot or more below the surface. Apparently at night and on dark cloudy days they venture out and roam about freely, for I have taken many trout whose stomach contents revealed the Alder Fly nymphs. (See the Catalogue for a pictorial representation of the larva.) After living in the water for approximately two years it crawls out and pupates in the earth on the banks of the stream. Two to three weeks later the adult fly may be noticed laying her eggs on the underside of bridges, spots so located that the larva when hatched fall directly into the water.

The larva of the Fish Fly, *Chauliodes serricornis,* is often mistaken for the Hellgrammite which it resembles, except that it is considerably smaller. Its habits are quite similar; that is, the larval stage is passed in the water, and pupation occurs on the land. Like the Alder Fly, the adult lays her eggs on the underside of bridges and on projecting rocks, so that the larvae, when hatched, fall directly down into the water.

Midge larvae are worm-like in form and live in thin filmy tubes attached to stones and leaves under water—sometimes at a great depth. There are two principal varieties, the white and the red; both are found on the slow moving trout streams, but the latter prefer lake regions, where they are known as

Nymphs

blood worms. Midge larvae are more or less nocturnal and at night often swim considerable distances from their homes with figure of eight lopings of their body. The length of the species varies from an eighth of an inch to almost an inch in length.

Within a few days after transformation from the larva, the pupa rises to the surface and floats there in a vertical position, descending when disturbed, but quickly rising again. The pupa usually remains within the tube constructed by the larva, but is capable of swimming about, much in the manner of a tadpole. Its most conspicuous feature in this stage is the hair-like gills, which resemble small silvery brushes (see the Catalogue for imitating this feature).

On lakes the empty pupa cases are a familiar sight, for the wind often collects them in thick scum-like patches, especially along the shore line. Both larva and pupa of the Midge are eagerly taken by trout, and they are among the most important insects that concern the fly fisher.

CHAPTER IV

Collecting Stream Insects

IN COLLECTING winged insects certain tools, such as a net, killing bottle, pins, etc., are needed.

The diameter of the net should be approximately ten to twelve inches and the depth of the bag about two times the diameter; the material should be of the finest and lightest cloth obtainable; and the handle should be about three feet long (see sketch).

The bottle containing the killing agent is constructed as follows: procure a wide mouthed bottle with a screw top. Place two layers of blotting paper on the bottom; over this blotting paper place a layer of cyanide of potassium about one-fourth of an inch thick; on top of the cyanide pour a thin layer of plaster of Paris about three-sixteenths of an inch thick; and finally on top of this place two more sheets of blotting paper. The bottle should at all times be tightly corked and should under no consideration be inhaled, for the fumes are exceedingly poisonous. After constructing such a bottle it should be allowed to age a week or so before being used. Insects should not remain long in the bottle and as soon as killed should be removed and pinned dry.

Pins for mounting may be procured from biological supply houses; they are about one-half inch long, have a small head, and are black enameled. Size No. 2 will prove about right for trout stream insects; and they are invariably pinned through the thorax. Mayflies should be mounted with wings close together in a vertical upright position; in pinning, endeavor not to crush the thorax.

A box must be prepared for housing the specimens. This can be an ordinary cigar box, rather deep, having a three-fourths inch layer of cork in the bottom. Assuming that the insect is as yet undetermined, a small sheet of paper should be pinned underneath the specimen, this paper to furnish the date and location (see sketch).

Another means of preserving insects is by dropping them into a bottle

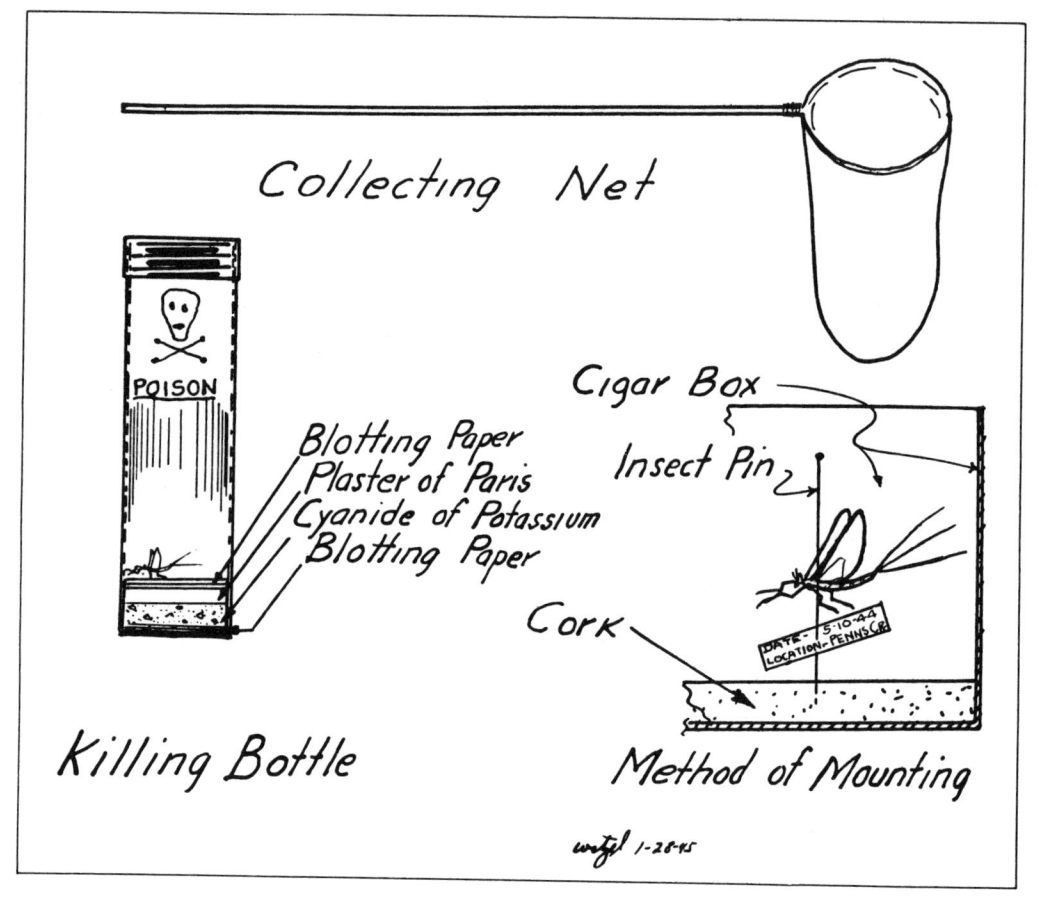

PLATE IV.

containing seventy per cent alcohol. A slip of paper written in pencil describing location and date should be put in with the insects for ready identification. Never use ink, for the writing will soon fade. The above alcohol solution is what is generally used by entomologists but is not too satisfactory; the colors will soon fade, in fact fading will occur in all insects preserved in any solution, regardless of what is used. The new, clear, colorless, liquid plastic material offers interesting possibilities. The insects are cast in a mold and it is claimed that the colors will not fade. For display purposes it would appear ideal; however, from an entomological angle its use might prove limited. Halford, in his *Modern Development of the Dry Fly* mentions a formalin solution, but the colors will fade in this almost as quickly as in alcohol. Be sure that the bottles used in housing the specimens are of large enough diameter, otherwise the flies will be crushed in withdrawing them for examination. In collecting specimens, I would urge that a considerable number be

Collecting Stream Insects

secured. In addition to those secured by the net, one can quite often pick them off spider webs and shrubbery bordering the stream. Collecting after dark can be accomplished by driving the car along the water's edge, spreading a white sheet on the front, and turning on the lights. Caddis flies and sub-imago Mayflies are especially attracted to lights, and it is a simple matter to pick them off the sheet and drop them into the bottle. By all means endeavor to procure flies on which trout are feeding, for without this assurance, the time and effort spent in catching them is definitely lost. Mayflies are found on almost every trout stream, and it is a simple matter to procure them with a net on any warm spring evening. During a hatch I have secured as many as twenty with one scoop of the net. Some Mayflies come out in almost unbelievable numbers, and I have seen them lying three and four inches deep the following day on bridges spanning the stream.

The Male of the Mayflies is preferred, since entomologists invariably record the male characteristics, which offer a ready means of indentification. The male fly can be recognized by the presence of a pair of claspers shaped like calipers on the end of its abdomen; he is also smaller than the female and has abnormally long front legs. If male and female can be secured in copula so much the better, for then the specific name of both sexes remains unquestioned. If the Mayflies are in the sub-imago stage, it is well in addition to the dead specimens, to secure a number alive and hold them over for a few days, awaiting their transformation to the spinner or imago stage. While awaiting this final moult, the sub-imago may be kept alive in a small cage made of window screening; a few damp leaves should be kept in the cage to insure proper moisture. After transforming to the spinner stage, the insects can then be killed, and if males are among the lot, no special trouble should be encountered in their identification. Thus by holding over such insects, one can secure both male and female specimens in both dun and spinner stages. I might mention that the dun or sub-imago can always be recognized by the fine hair around the wing borders and by its dull colored wings. This hair can only be noticed with the aid of a magnifying glass. If the wings are clear and sparkling, the Mayfly is undoubtedly a spinner or imago.

Entomologists are usually glad to receive specimens for determination, and none of them charge anything for this service. Many will provide you with bottles containing a solution for their preservation and for shipping. Put in a request that half the specimens be returned to you.

In shipping pinned specimens, the original container, that is a cork lined box, should be packed in excelsior in another larger box, so that the specimens will not be injured. Those preserved in a solution should have the bottles filled full to the cork so that no splashing or jarring will result. These bottles may be housed in an inner box filled with sawdust. The package may be sent parcel post, and it should be labeled "Museum Specimens—May Be Opened For Postal Inspection If Required."

The study of entomology is very fascinating. I have spent many hours over it, but it requires considerable time and study before one can hope to trace the fly down to its specific name. And even when it has been verified by an expert in that field, the chances are that it will be given an entirely new name sometime during the next twenty years.

Entomologists are divided roughly into two groups: Splitters and Lumpers. The Splitters endeavor to give a new name to practically every fly, even though it has already been correctly figured and recorded; the Lumpers, on the other hand, try to maintain the original name of the fly, and any slight deviations from the original description are disregarded. Examples of such deviations occur in the large Grey Drakes, *Ephemera guttulata,* which on Spring Creek in Pennsylvania, grow to a somewhat larger size than those found elsewhere; another is the Red Quill, *Iron pleuralis*. This fly, commonly found on Eastern streams is also somewhat larger and darker than the recorded specimen, and many entomologists would classify it as *Iron fraudator*. Be that as it may, what we are particularly interested in is the color and description of the insect, not so much its name; and some of the names given to these flies are humdingers.

I recall one evening at the Academy of Natural Sciences when a certain distinguished entomologist was reading his paper on the description of a new species.

"I have named this fly—*S-S-S-S-c-c-c-c-S-S-S-c-c-c-Sc-Sc-Sc-.*"

After stuttering a few more minutes, the Doctor rather sheepishly said: "It's a rather difficult name to pronounce; perhaps I had better spell it."

Which he did, amid much applause!

CHAPTER V

Scientific Stream Entomology

THE BODY of an insect is divided into three parts, the head, thorax, and abdomen. On the head of the insect appears the feelers or antennae, the palps or tasting organs, the mouth parts, and the eyes—both simple and compound. (See anatomical sketch of stone fly nymph.)

The thorax is divided into three segments, the prothorax, the mesothorax, and the metathorax. That part of the thorax which bears the front legs is called the prothorax; the middle leg section is the mesothorax; and the hind leg section the metathorax. The back of the thorax is termed the notum and the underside the sternum; thus we have pronotum, prosternum, mesonotum, mesosternum, etc. The sides are called pleura, and again we have mesoplerum, metaplerum, etc. If the insect has two pairs of wings, the front pair is attached to the mesothorax and the rear pair to the metathorax; if there should be only one pair, it is on the mesothorax.

The wings are composed of two layers of integument traversed by veins and nervures, and the location and arrangement of these veins are most important in determining family, genus, and species. Among the Diptera, or two winged insects, the hind wings are very much atrophied and are usually present in the form of very small, knob-like appendages, called halters. Among the crane flies these knobs are very clearly defined.

Insects always have six legs and the principal parts are the coxa, the trochanter, the femur, the tibia, and the tarsus or foot. The relative length of these component parts are again useful in determining certain species. The big joints of the leg are the femur and tibia.

The abdomen is generally composed of eleven segments or less, and often terminated by caudal appendages such as the cerci of the *Ephemeroptera* and the ovipositor of the *Hymenoptera*. Each abdominal segment is ring-like and composed of a tergite (the dorsal half) and a sternite (the ventral half), which meet on the sides. Taken collectively, the back segments are known as tergites as opposed to the belly sternites. Starting from the meta-

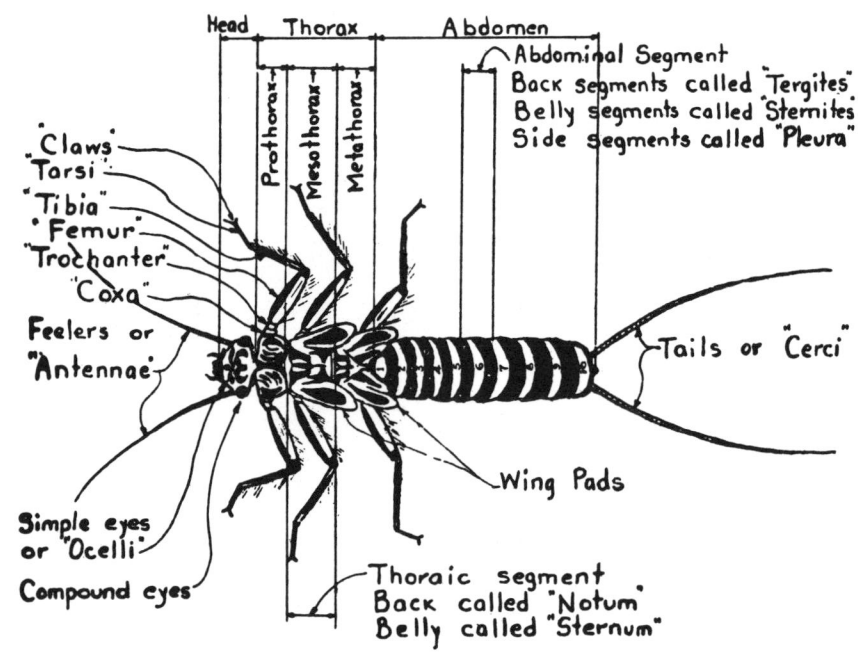

ANATOMICAL SKETCH OF STONE FLY NYMPH

PLATE V.

thorax and progressing towards the caudal end, we will number the segments 1, 2, 3, 4, etc. (see sketch). Sutures are lines separating the body walls, and any such areas bounded by sutures are known as sclerites. The external skin or covering of an insect is composed of a tough, flexible, horn-like substance called chitin.

Determining the specific name of an insect is in many cases impossible, especially among females. Mayflies in the sub-imago stage are another source of trouble, since the available data records only the adult male characteristics. The male fly offers the readiest solution, since quite often the final determination hinges on the male genitalia. Preparing a genitalic slide is quite a task, especially for amateurs; in fact, when it becomes necessary to resort to it, the insect should be sent to some authority for verification. As I have mentioned, many insects can be readily and accurately determined from the location and arrangement of the wing veins, lengths of the various parts of the legs, and other characteristics. Naturally one must have a monograph on the order, and by closely studying and following the keys, the amateur can finally trace it down to its specific name.

Scientific Stream Entomology 31

A good glass is absolutely essential. I have a Bausch and Lomb, No. 14X, Hastings Triplet; the diameter is smaller than a dime, yet it is remarkably powerful, and will bring out the necessary details in following the keys.

In cases where the wing venation is rather difficult, I generally snip off the wing, place it between two microscopic slides, and then fasten the edges together with adhesive tape. The slide is then placed under a projector, which in a dark room throws a large image on a sheet of paper; then the wing can be traced off and the veins lettered. The sketches showing the three great families of Mayflies, *Baetidae, Heptageniidae,* and the *Ephemeridae* were prepared in this way.

One naturally must know and recognize the principal veins, the Costa, C; the subcosta, Sc; the Radius, R; the Media, M; the cubitus, Cu; and the Anal veins, A. In general it is a complicated and fascinating study, and the field is so large that one should not dabble in the various orders, but should confine his activities to one group; and in that one group, one should get every monograph and all the available literature on the subject.

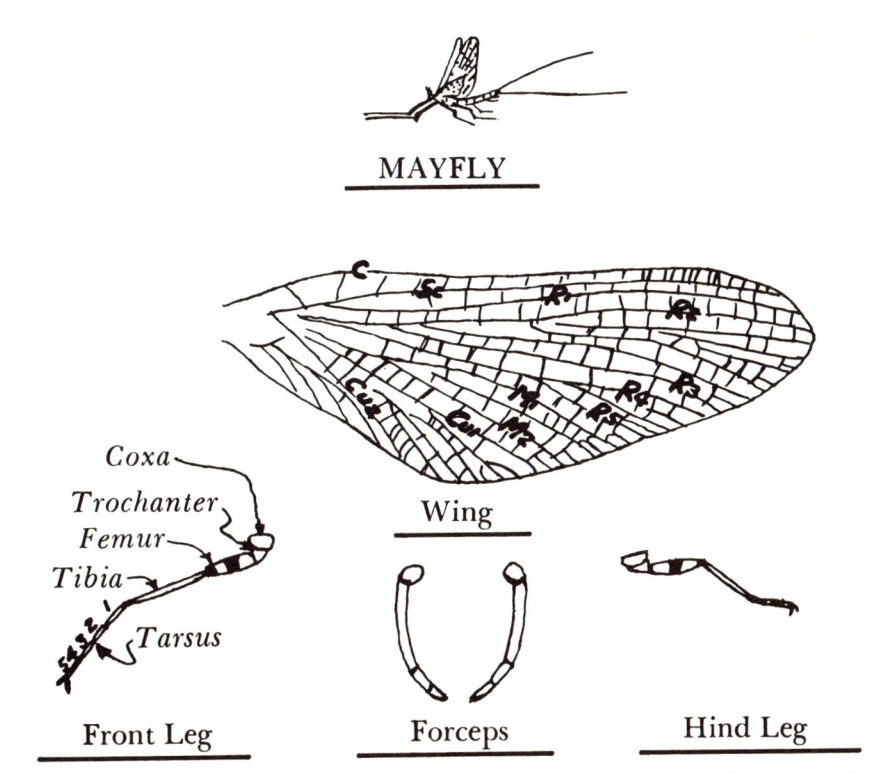

MAYFLY

Front Leg — Coxa, Trochanter, Femur, Tibia, Tarsus

Wing

Forceps

Hind Leg

PLATE VI. Mayfly taken on Young Woman's Creek, Pa., April 15. All details greatly enlarged.

In describing insects, entomologists invariably use the metric system, and for small trout stream insects like those hereinafter described, the unit of measure is the millimeter. For ready conversion all one needs to keep in mind is that 25.4 millimeters equals one inch. I have converted these figures into inches and fractions of an inch when describing the natural flies.

And now that we have gained a general idea of those flies and insects interesting to trout as fish food, suppose we delve a little deeper into the subject, insofar as it pertains to a more specific identification.

To illustrate the method of procedure in tracing down an insect to its specific name, suppose we take the case of a Mayfly we have just caught on Young Womans Creek on the opening day (April 15) of the trout fishing season.

This particular insect is a male fly, which is apparent from the claspers or forceps, and it is in the spinner or imago stage, having clear glassy wings. The abdomen is reddish brown; legs, pale reddish brown with prominent black spots on each femur; tails, deep reddish brown, two in number; length of wings, three-eighths to seven-sixteenths of an inch, corresponding to about 10 to 11 millimeters. A sketch of the insect, together with enlarged details of its wings, legs, etc. is shown above. It will be assumed that the angler is sufficiently familiar with those insects found over the water to determine the order, which for the Mayfly group is *Ephemeroptera*.

The second step is to determine what family the insect belongs to. To do this, one should have access to a monograph on the *Ephemeroptera*. Dr. James G. Needham of Cornell University, the senior author of the *Biology of Mayflies,* has granted me permission to reproduce the following keys from that monumental work, and I wish at this time to acknowledge my thanks for his kindness.

NORTH AMERICAN MAYFLIES
ORDER EPHEMEROPTERA

These are winged insects of moderate size and incomplete metamorphosis whose immature stages are aquatic, whose adult life is very brief, and whose characteristics are more fully set forth in the preceding pages of this volume. They are found in all fresh waters in every part of North America, and are among the most important of herbivorous invertebrate aquatic animals.

They may be grouped in three main families, distinguished as follows:

KEY TO THE FAMILIES OF EPHEMEROPTERA
Adults

1—Veins M and Cu 1 strongly divergent at base, with M 2 strongly bent toward Cu basally. Outer fork (Of) in hind wing wanting. Hind tarsi 4-jointed ....EPHEMERIDAE

—Veins M and Cu 1 little divergent at base and fork of M more nearly symmetrical. Outer fork (Of) of Rs in hind wing present or absent. Hind tarsus 4- or 5-jointed 2

2—Hind tarsus with five freely movable joints. Cubital intercalaries in two parallel pairs, long and short alternately. Venation never greatly reduced. Eyes of the male simple. ....................HEPTAGENIIDAE

—Hind tarsi with three or four freely movable joints. Cubital intercalaries not as above (except in Metretopinae). Venation sometimes greatly reduced. Eyes of the male often divided. ....BAETIDAE

From an inspection of the above key, we can see that the Mayflies are divided into three great families. Just what family our Mayfly belongs to, we shall now attempt to determine.

In using the keys, start with the number I, at the left top. Read both characteristics; determine which one applies to the insect; then go to the number given. To illustrate: If veins M and Cur1 are little divergent at the base....2, go to 2 on left above and continue in like manner.

From a study of the wing of the insect, on which I have indicated the principal veins, i.e., the Costa C, the subcosta Sc, the radius R, the Media M, the Cubitus Cu, and the Anal veins A, it is apparent that veins M and Cur1 are a little divergent at the base. So, we will continue on to 2.

From the enlarged detail of the insect's leg, we note that the hind tarsus has five freely movable joints; another inspection of the wing reveals that the cubal intercalaries are in two parallel pairs, long and short alternately. These characteristics correspond with our Mayfly and definitely place it as belonging to the family *Heptageniidae*. Our next problem is to determine the genus from the key given below.

KEY TO GENERA OF HEPTAGENINAE
Adults

1—Outer fork (Of) of Rs (R_{4+5}) of hind wing wanting male forceps 5-jointed .... Arthroplea
—Outer fork of Rs of hind wing present; male forceps 4-jointed 2
2—Fore tarsus of male not more than 3/4 as long as tibia; apical margin of forceps base deeply excavated .... Anepeorus
—Fore tarsus of male distinctly longer than tibia; apical margin of forceps base not as above 3
3—Basal joint of fore tarsus of male 1/2 or less than 1/2 as long as second joint 4
—Basal joint of fore tarsus of male at least 2/3 as long as second joint, may equal or slightly exceed it in length 6
4—Stigmatic cross veins more or less anastomosed; basal joint of fore tarsus of male 1/6 to 1/4 as long as second .... Rhithrogena
—Stigmatic cross veins not anastomosed; basal joint of fore tarsus of male variable 5
5—Basal joint of fore tarsus of male 1/3 to 1/2 as long as second; penes more or less distinctly L-shaped .... Stenonema
—Basal joint of fore tarsus of male 1/6 to 1/3 as long as second; penes not distinctly L-shaped .... Heptagenia
6—Basal joint of fore tarsus of male 2/3 to 3/4 as long as second joint ... 7
—Basal joint of fore tarsus of male equal to or slightly longer than second joint 8
7—Stigmatic area of fore wing divided by a fine line into an upper and lower series of cellules; basal costal cross veins very weak .... Cinygma
—Stigmatic area of fore wing not divided as above; basal costal cross veins usually well developed .... Cinygmula
8—Stigmatic cross veins of fore wing more or less strongly anastomosed, sometimes forming two series of cellules; basal costal cross veins weak .... Ironopsis
—Stigmatic cross veins of fore wing not anastomosed; basal costal cross veins variable 9
9—Basal costal cross veins of fore wing weak; stigmatic cross veins not slanting .... Iron
—Basal costal cross veins of fore wing strong; stigmatic cross veins distinctly slanting .... Ironodes

Starting at 1 on the left top, the first similar characteristics noted are that the male forceps or claspers are four-jointed. Continue to 2, where it is seen that the fore tarsus of the male is longer than the tibia. Continue to 3, wherein we note that the basal joint of the fore tarsus of the male is as long or slightly longer than the second joint. Continue to 6, where this is definitely confirmed. At 8 we check the fact that the stigmatic cross veins on the front wing are not anastomosed. In 9, we see from the wing that the basal cross veins of the fore wing are weak, which places it in the genus *Iron*. As a further check, verify it by the verification table given below.

VERIFICATION TABLE
Adults

Genus	Basal costal cross-veins	stigmat. c. vs. Slant Anast.[1]	Claws[2] of ♂	Forc. joints.	♂ eyes contig.
Anepeorus[3]	Rather weak	Yes	Part.	Similar	4	No
Arthroplea[4]	Rather weak	No	No	Dissim.	5	Almost
Cinygma	Weak	Yes	Fully	Dissim.	4	No
Cinygmula	Strong	Yes	No	Var.	4	No
Heptagenia	Var.	No	No	Dissim.	4	No
Iron	Weak	No	No	Var.	4	Usually
Ironodes	Strong	Yes	No	Dissim.	4	No
Ironopsis	Weak	Yes	Fully	Dissim.	4	Yes
Rhithrogena	Rather weak	Yes	Part.	Dissim.	4	Usually
Stenonema	Strong	Var.	No	Dissim.	4	No

[1] Stigmatic cross veins anastomosed partially Part) or fully, forming two complete rows of cells.
[2] Fore claws, male tarsus.
[3] Fore tarsus of male shorter than tibia.
[4] Second branch of radial sector (O₂) not forked.

Before proceeding with the determination of the specific name of the insect, suppose we read what the *Biology of Mayflies* has to say concerning the genus *Iron*.

GENUS IRON EATON

1883—Eaton—Revis. Monogr. Pl. 24, fig. 44.
1885—Eaton—Revis. Monogr. p. 244.
1905—Needham—Bull. N. Y. St. Mus. 86:53.
1920—Ulmer—Stett. Ent. Zeit. 81:142 (also Epeorus, in part.)
1924—McDunnough—Canad. Ent. 56:129.
1933—Traver—J. Elisha Mitchell Sci. Soc. 48:156.
1933—Traver—J. N. Y. Ent. Soc. 41:116.
1933—Spieth—J. N. Y. Ent. Soc. 41:330.

Mayflies of small to medium size, ranging in length of wing from 7 to 11 mm. Eyes of male large, usually contiguous apically. Posterior margin of head of female very slightly emarginate. Posterior margin of pronotum somewhat excavated in median area. Fore leg of male as long as or slightly longer than body. In the type species, fore femur of male about 2/3 as long as tibia, which is about ¾ the length of tarsus. Basal joint of fore tarsus as long as or slightly longer than 2nd joint; 3rd subequal to 2nd; 4th slightly shorter than 3rd; 5th about ½ as long as 4th. Fore femur of female only slightly shorter than tibia; tarsus subequal to femur. Basal fore tarsal joint fully ¾ of 2nd joint; 3rd and 5th subequal to 1st; 4th about ½ of 2nd. In hind leg of both sexes, femur about ¾ as long as tibia; tarsus about ½ as long as femur. Basal tarsal joint subequal to or very slightly longer than 2nd; 3rd and 4th progressively shorter; 5th about equal to 1st and 2nd combined. In most species, a prominent black mark is present at middle of each femur. Claws dissimilar on all tarsi, in both sexes, except in species of the *albertae* group, in which claws of male fore tarsus are similar and blunt. Typical Heptagenine venation. Cross veins of stigmatic area not anastomosed. In many species, basal costal cross veins weak and indistinct; in species of the *albertae* and *humeralis* groups*, the

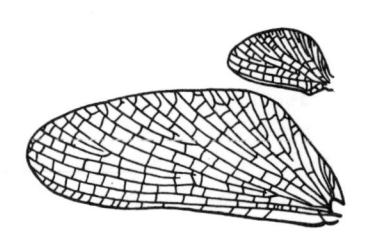

PLATE VII. Wings of *Iron fragilis* (drawing by Anna H. Morgan).

humeral cross vein is thickened and black in its posterior portion. Second fork of radial sector in hind wing arises basad of first fork.

Apical margin of forceps base saliently produced, in species of the *longimanus* and *pleuralis* types, and in *I. deceptivus*; in the *humeralis* group this margin is more or less regularly undulate, while in the *albertae* group it may be slightly emarginate or somewhat produced. Forceps four-jointed, second joint longest. Fourth joint slightly shorter than third, these two combined being shorter than second joint. Penes united in basal 2/3 of their length (except in *I. deceptivus*). A pair of median spines is typically present; these are much reduced in the *humeralis* group, and wanting in *I. modestus* and in the *pleuralis* group. Long stout pick-shaped lateral spines occur in *I. pleuralis* and in *I. proprius;* shorter lateral spines are typically present in the other groups (absent in *I. modestus* and *I. deceptivus*). Apical margin of subanal plate of female emarginate in median area.

* In a previous paper (J. N. Y. Ent. Soc. 41:118; 1933) I have used the term *nitidus* group; since *nitidus* Etn. has been transferred to another genus, I now refer to this as the *humeralis* group. The *albertae* and *pleuralis* groups are now recognized as distinct types. My reference to *pleuralis* in that paper applies to *fraudator* n. sp.; the reference to *modestus* should be disregarded, as further evidence indicates that I had mis-identified that species.—J. R. T.

We have now determined the order, family, and genus of the trout stream insect, and it still remains to identify it as to species. Continue on in like manner with the keys.

KEY TO THE SPECIES
Male Adults*

1—Genitalia of the *albertae* type (see fig. 107); fore claws of male usually similar, blunt 2
— Genitalia not as above; fore claws of male dissimilar 6
2—No distinct blackish markings on thoracic pleura 3
— Thoracic pleura with distinct blackish markings 4
3—Fore femur and tibia subequal; median spines on penes rather stout, relatively short; apical margin of forceps base somewhat excavated laterally (see fig. 107) ....albertae
—Fore femur shorter than tibia; median spines on penes longer and more slender; apical margin of forceps base slightly convex (see fig. 107) ....lagunitas
4—Abdominal segments 2-7 yellowish, tergites may be faintly smoky; apical margin of the forceps base somewhat produced; venation variable 5
—Abdominal segments 2-7 whitish, with pale brownish markings; apical margin of forceps base somewhat excavated laterally (see fig. 107); venation pale, most cross veins indistinct ....youngi
5—Venation brown, all cross veins distinct; penes as in fig. 107 ....
....sancta-gabriel
— Venation pale, cross veins mostly indistinct; penes, as in fig. 107 ....
....dulciana
6—Genitalia of the *pleuralis* type (see fig. 106) 7
— Genitalia not as above 8
7—Oblique lateral black streak on each tergite, cutting across postero-lateral angle; penes as in fig. 106 ....pleuralis
—No such oblique lateral black streak on tergites ....proprius
8—Genitalia of the *longimanus* type (see fig. 105) 9
— Genitalia not as above 13
9—Wing 7-8 mm. in length 10
— Wing 9-11 mm. in length 11
10—Apical margin of forceps base regularly sinuate (see fig. 105); no oblique dark streak across postero-lateral angle of tergites ......tenuis
—Apical margin of forceps base extended forward more at median line than laterally; oblique black streak across postero-lateral angle of each tergite ....fragilis
11—Thorax and abdomen largely dark red-brown; venation dark brown ..
....fraudator
— Thorax and abdomen largely tinged with light red-brown; venation pale brown 12
12—Black posterior margins of tergites extend laterally to pleural fold ....
....confusus
— Black posterior margins of tergites do not extend to pleural fold, but an oblique black line from this margin cuts across postero-lateral triangle to pleural fold ....longimanus

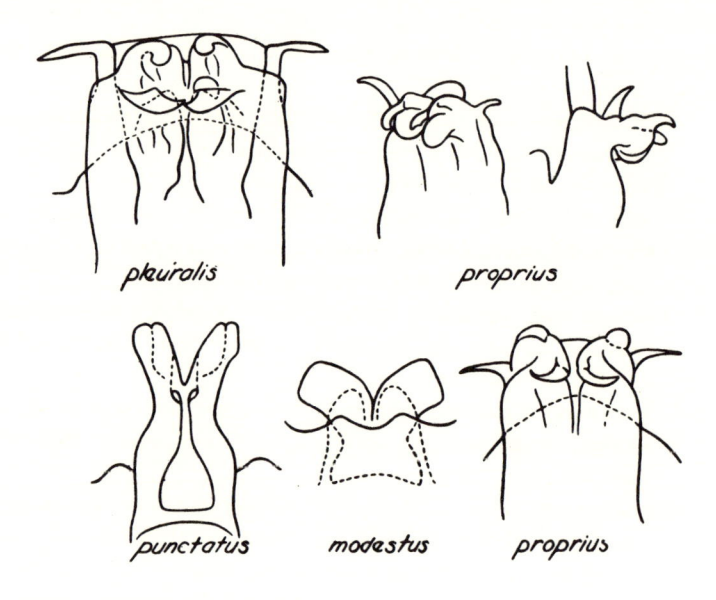

PLATE VIII. Male genitalia of four species of Iron; three views of *proprius* (*punctatus*, after McDunnough).

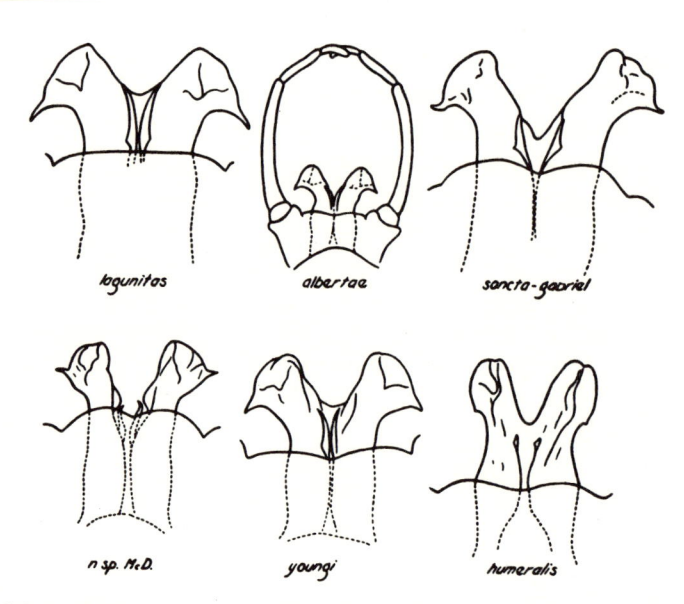

PLATE IX. Male genitalia of six species of Iron (drawing designated "n.sp. McD." is *I. dulciana* McD.; named after this drawing was prepared).

13—Genitalia of the *humeralis* type (see fig. 106, *punctatus*) 14
 —Genitalia not of the *humeralis* type 18
14—Apical margin of forceps base as in fig. 105; venation light brown ..
 .... dispar
 —Apical margin of forceps base more regularly undulate, as in fig. 106;
   venation whitish or pale yellowish 15
15—Wing 8-9 mm. in length 16
 —Wing 10-11 mm. in length 17
16—Thorax blackish brown; no small lateral spines on outer margin of
   penes; eyes not contiguous apically .... punctatus
 —Thorax pale yellowish brown; small lateral spines present on outer
   margin of penes, but not conspicuous; eyes contiguous apically ....
   .... rubidus
17—Thorax dull brown, abdominal tergites suffused with brown; penes
   longer and more widely separated apically than in following
   species .... suffusus
 —Thorax yellowish, often with oblique dark markings on pleura; abdominal tergites typically much paler than above ...... humeralis
18—Penes short and stout, spines lacking (see fig. 106); tails pale, joinings
   distinctly dark; femora with median and apical bands .... modestus
 —Penes longer and more slender, with long medium spines (see fig. 105);
   tails dark, joinings not distinct; femora unmarked .... deceptivus

No genitalic slide will be made, but so far as these organs are visible, they do not check with the *alberta* type. Continue to 6, where a similarity is found to the *pleuralis* type. Continue to 7, where both characteristics coincide with the *pleuralis* species. As a further check consult the Verification Table given on the following page,

VERIFICATION TABLE
Male Adults*

Species	Wing length	Venation	Dk. mks. pleura	Tergites 2 to 7	Genital type of	Distr.
albertae	11	Brown	No	Smoky	Albert.**	W
confusus	10-11	Pale br.	Few	Red-br.	Longim.	N. Y.
deceptivus	9-10	Dk. br.	No	Brown	Decept.	W
dispar	9	Lght. br.	Yes	Yellow	Humeral.	N. C.
fragilis	7	Pale	No	Yellow	Longim.	E
fraudator	10-11	Dk. br.	No	Dk. br.	Longim.	E
hesperus	12	Yellow	Yes	Pale	?	Wash.
humeralis	10-11	Whitish	Yes	Whitish	Humeral.	E
lagunitas	11	Lght. br.	No	Yellow	Albert.	Calif.
longimanus	11	Lght. br.	No	Brown	Longim.	W
modestus	7	Pale br.	No?	Pale	Modest.	Md.
pleuralis	10-12	Dk. br.	No	Dk. br.	Pleural.	N. Y.
proprius	10	Lght. br.	No	Pale br.	Pleural.	Colo.
punctatus	8	Pale	No	Whitish	Humeral.	E
rubidus	8-9	Yellow	Yes	Whitish	Humeral.	N. C.
sancta-gabriel	10½	Brown	Yes	Yellow	Albert.	Calif.
suffusus	11	Pale	No	Brown	Humeral.	E
tenuis	8	Pale	Yes	Whitish	Longim.	N. Y.
youngi	10-11	Pale br.	Yes	Whitish	Albert.	Ore.
dulciana	9½	Pale	Yes	Yellow	Albert.	B. C.

Since the characteristics all agree, we may tentatively assume that the specific name is *pleuralis*. Now let us read the entomologist's description of *Iron pleuralis*:

IRON PLEURALIS BANKS

1910—Banks—Canad. Ent. 42:102. Fig. (Heptagenia [Epeorus]) ....N. Y.
Length: body 9-10, wing 10-11 mm.

A reddish brown species; cross veins of basal costal space indistinct; genitalia of *pleuralis* type, having a long prominent lateral spine on each side of penes.

A paratype of this species presented to the Cornell collection by Dr. Banks, is the basis for this description. Several other specimens in Dr. Banks' collection, taken at the same time and place and associated with *I. pleuralis*, prove to be *Rhithrogena jejuna*, as indicated by Dr. Banks' notes in his correspondence with us, and by a specimen which he kindly lent us for study. It is probable that the original description included both this species and *R. jejuna*.

Head of male reddish brown; no distinct markings. Thorax quite uniform dark red-brown; pronotum shaded with smoky brown except on anterior margin. No such distinct paler markings anterior to wing root and on pleura, as indicated in original description. Legs pale reddish brown. Fore leg longer than body. Basal fore tarsal joint subequal to second, third almost as long. A prominent black spot near median area of each femur. Apical margin of each trochanter very narrowly blackish; faint indications of a small darker spot at each apical angle. Basal joint of hind tarsus slightly longer than second joint. Middle and hind tarsi somewhat darker than their respective tibiae. Wings hyaline, seemingly with very faint yellowish tinge; hardly darker in stigmatic area. (Original description does not mention yellowish tinge, but states, "rather darker in costal area near the tip." Discrepancy may be due to fact that paratype has been in alcohol presumably since date of capture). Basal costal cross veins very faint; about 6 before the bulla. Four or five immediately following bulla are likewise very faint. Stigmatic cross veins heavier, distinct; about 14 in number. Venation light brown; longitudinal veins very slightly heavier than cross veins.

Abdominal segments 2-8 semi-hyaline; 9 and 10 largely opaque. Light reddish brown in color, with a yellow tinge; tergites barely darker than sternites. Tergites 2-7 with a paler brownish median area, short submedian streaks from anterior margin which may coalesce with the pale median streak; anterior margins and antero-lateral angles likewise paler brown. A distinct blackish streak at spiracular area, extending from posterior margin in a curve to the pleural fold, cutting off postero-lateral angle. Small pale brownish spot faintly indicated at ganglionic area of each sternite. Penes with two dorsally-directed lobes (best seen in side view) apically near median area; below these on dorsal side, a curved chitinized structure; on each side, a prominent laterally-directed spine-like process (see fig. 106). Distinctly different from genitalia of the *longimanus* type; adults may be readily confused with species of the latter type in their general appearance.

There are several local specimens in the Cornell collection, some pinned and others in alcohol, in which the genitalia are very similar to the above paratype of *I. pleuralis*. These have a somewhat paler mesonotum, and greyish areas anterior to wing root and on pleura, most evident in alcoholic specimens; more distinct black dots at apical angles of each trochanter. Wing with no yellow tinge, but slightly darker in stigmatic area; venation deeper brown; no pale median areas as on tergites, other pale areas as in Dr. Banks' specimen; tergites dark red-brown, distinctly darker than sternites, which are tinged with brown. Tails deep red-brown. We are considering these to be *I. pleuralis*.

Previous references to *I. pleuralis* in the literature by McDunnough, Ide, Traver and others seem to apply rather to *I. fraudator*, with which species the true *pleuralis* has been confused. The western *I. proprius* is the only other known species having genitalia of the *pleuralis* type; it differs from *I. pleuralis* in its somewhat smaller size and in details of the structure of the penes.

EPHEMERIDAE

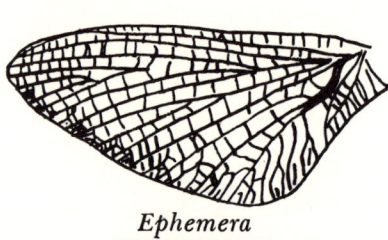

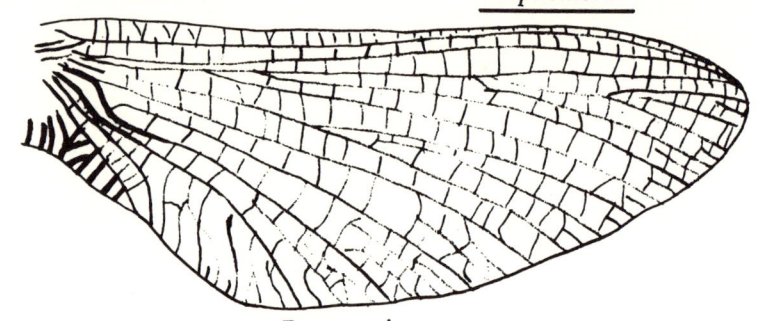

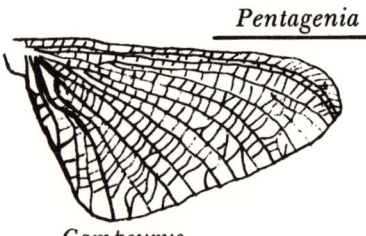

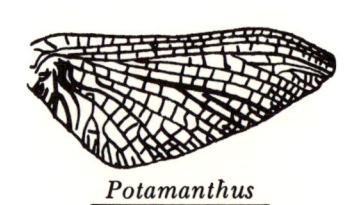

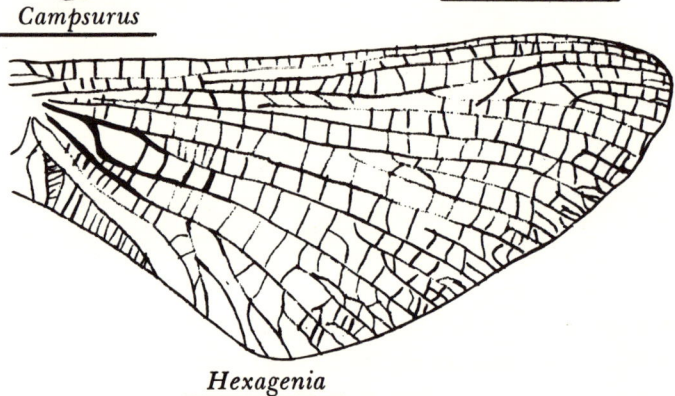

Ephoron

Ephemera

Pentagenia

Campsurus

Potamanthus

Hexagenia

PLATE X. Wings of Mayflies—Family *Ephemeridae*.

In reading over the above description we find that there are so many points of similarity that there no longer remains much doubt as to the insect being *Iron pleuralis*. Thus we have it completely identified, and summing it all up, we arrive at the following:

Order—*Ephemeroptera*   Genus—*Iron*
Family—*Heptageniidae*   Species—*pleuralis*

In angling parlance this insect is known as the Red Quill Spinner, and is one of the earliest Mayflies to appear over the trout streams. Jennings and Flick call it the Quill Gordon; however, I believe the name to be questionable (see chapter 9 on the Quill Gordon). Typically it is a cold water fly and may be noticed about mid-day in the warm bright sunshine, rising and falling over the water. While descending in this rhythmic aerial flight, the two tails of the insect are extended out at right angles to the body and serve as a brake. Very few flies are feeding on the surface when this insect first appears in early spring, and for that reason the artificial tied as a wet fly will prove the most efficacious. The Red Quill, when fished wet, has accounted for many trout, and it can be recommended as being one of the best for fishing cold water mountain brooks.

And now that the reader has gained a general idea as to how to identify a Mayfly, it might be well to study the wing venation of the three principal families, i.e. the *Ephemeridae, Baetidae* and *Heptageniidae*, see Plate X. Veins characteristic of the genus are drawn heavy and full. While not all of the wings of the various genera are illustrated, it is believed that those shown are among the most common varieties and embrace the majority of those most frequently encountered over the water.

Almost every trout stream harbors Mayflies, and the fly fisher will reap rich rewards by tying up artificials imitating those which have no counterpart in his fly book. After one becomes insect conscious, and spends some time in observation, he will note many insects that bear a startling resemblance to some of the old time favorite fly patterns in his fly book. Chief among the latter is the Pink Lady.

I imagine that the majority of us know how the Pink Lady originated, for it is charmingly told in that angling classic, *The Dry Fly and Fast Water*. George La Branche, who had fished the King of Waters unsuccessfully the day before, discovered on the following morning that a great deal of the red dye used upon the silk body of the fly had come off on the drying pad, causing the body to change from red to a beautiful pink. The pink bodied fly proved a killer on that day and on many succeeding days, and was dubbed the Pink Lady by one of his friends. This fly has weathered the test of time,

HEPTAGENIIDAE

Heptagenia

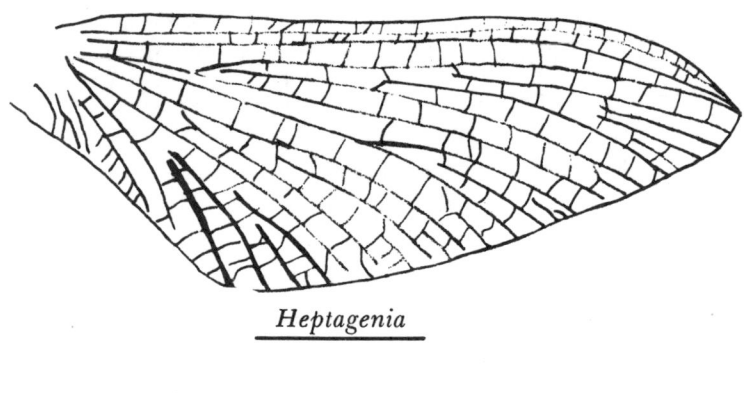

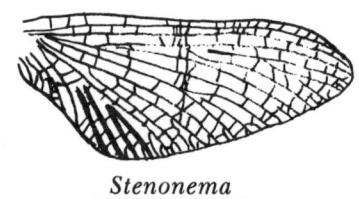

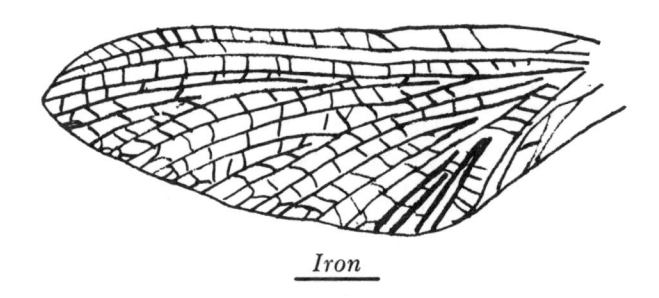

Stenonema

Iron

PLATE XI. Wings of Mayflies—Family *Heptageniidae*.

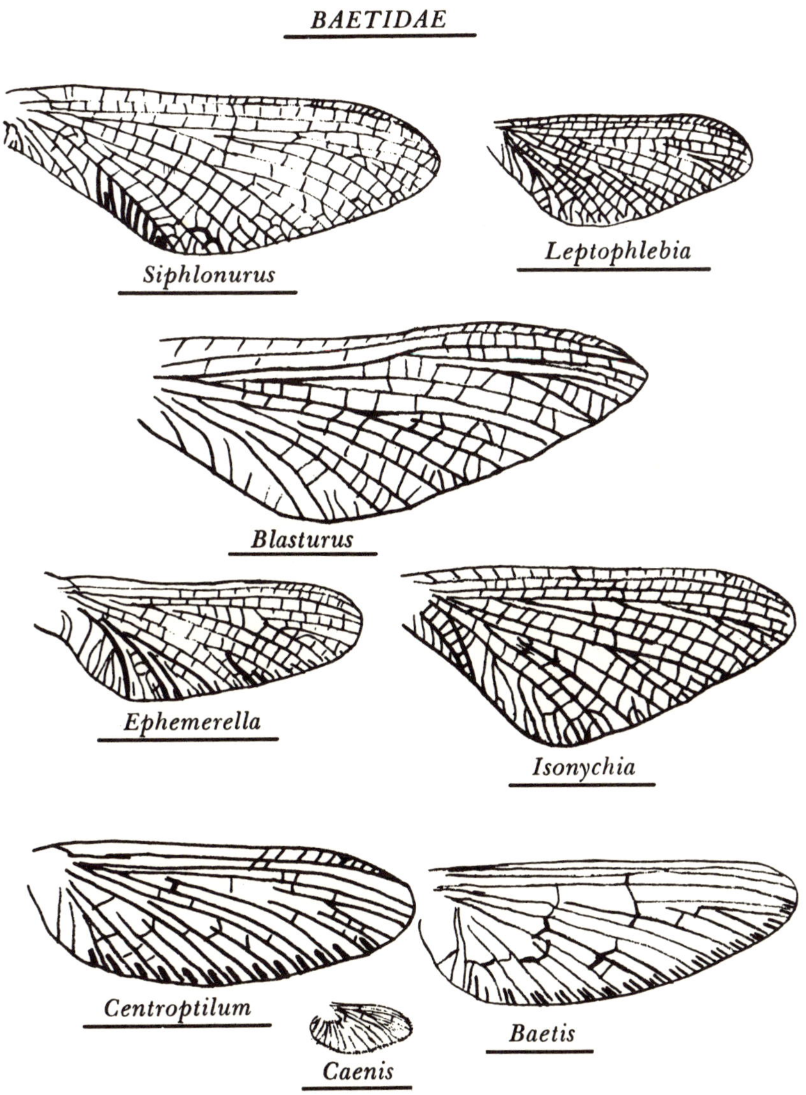

PLATE XII. Wings of Mayflies—Family *Baetidae*.

but I have often wondered if its success is not due in a great measure to the strong resemblance it bears to one of the Heptageniidae mayflies in the dun or sub-imago stage. Why I hold this view is related in the next paragraph.

One evening while fishing on the Brodheads, I chanced to find the trout rising well to a pink bodied mayfly. The insect was in the sub-imago stage, and noticing the close resemblance to the Pink Lady, I decided to capture a few, hold them over until they reached the spinner or image stage, and then determine the specific name. However, my good intentions came to naught, for the insects, hastily placed in my dry fly box among the artificials, were found crushed and dead the following morning when I chanced to remember the incident. They had not yet shed the sub-imago skin, making identification impossible; and while a cursory glance at the wing venation placed them among the *Heptageniidae*, that was as far as the investigation proceeded. This insect undoubtedly developed into the White Mayfly—with its pink egg sack, *Stenonema rubromaculatum*—which was over the water in good numbers the following day.

Some time ago, while at The Angler's Club in New York, I mentioned to La Branche that I believed the Pink Lady's success could be attributed to the fact that it had a living prototype, and he concurred with this thought immediately. He had for a long time entertained such an opinion—though without definite proof—and we both regretted that the insect's identity was never definitely established. Perhaps in time, some future fly fishing entomologist will shed more light on this matter.

CHAPTER VI

The Catalog

LITTLE BLACK STONE FLY

Order—*Plecoptera* Genus—*Taeniopteryx*
Family—*Nemouridae* Species—*fasciata*

DESCRIPTION: Length to tip of wings, 7/16 to 5/8 of an inch. General color, blackish. Antennae, black; wings, blackish brown; abdomen, dark brown; tails, short and yellowish; legs, dark blackish brown.

REMARKS: This is one of the earliest flies to appear during the trout fishing season, and I have seen them out when the snow was still on the ground. They favor rather cold days, but as soon as the weather becomes mild they disappear. I usually tie and fish this fly wet because early in the season not enough insects are abroad to cause trout to rise to the surface.

IMITATION: Hook, No. 16; wings, crow; body, dubbing of black and brown wool; hackle, black; tail, two short wisks of black hackle fibres.

* * * *

LITTLE BLACK CADDIS

Order—*Trichoptera* Genus—*Chimarrha*
Family—*Philopotamidae* Species—*atterima*

DESCRIPTION: Length to tip of wings, 1/4 to 5/16 of an inch. Wings, blackish, mainly due to fine dark brown microscopic hair; body, black; legs, dark brown; tails, none; antennae, black.

REMARKS: The larva of this fly is one of the net spinning caddis worms. These nets, about one inch long and one-eighth of an inch wide, are fastened at the lower front end to stones and serve the purpose of collecting food for the larva which lives within. The pupa lies in a case of small stones, which like many others are fastened to larger rocks in the stream bed. *Chimarrha atterima* emerges from its case quite early in the season and is one of the earliest caddis flies to appear over the water. Unlike the majority of the

PLATE XIII.

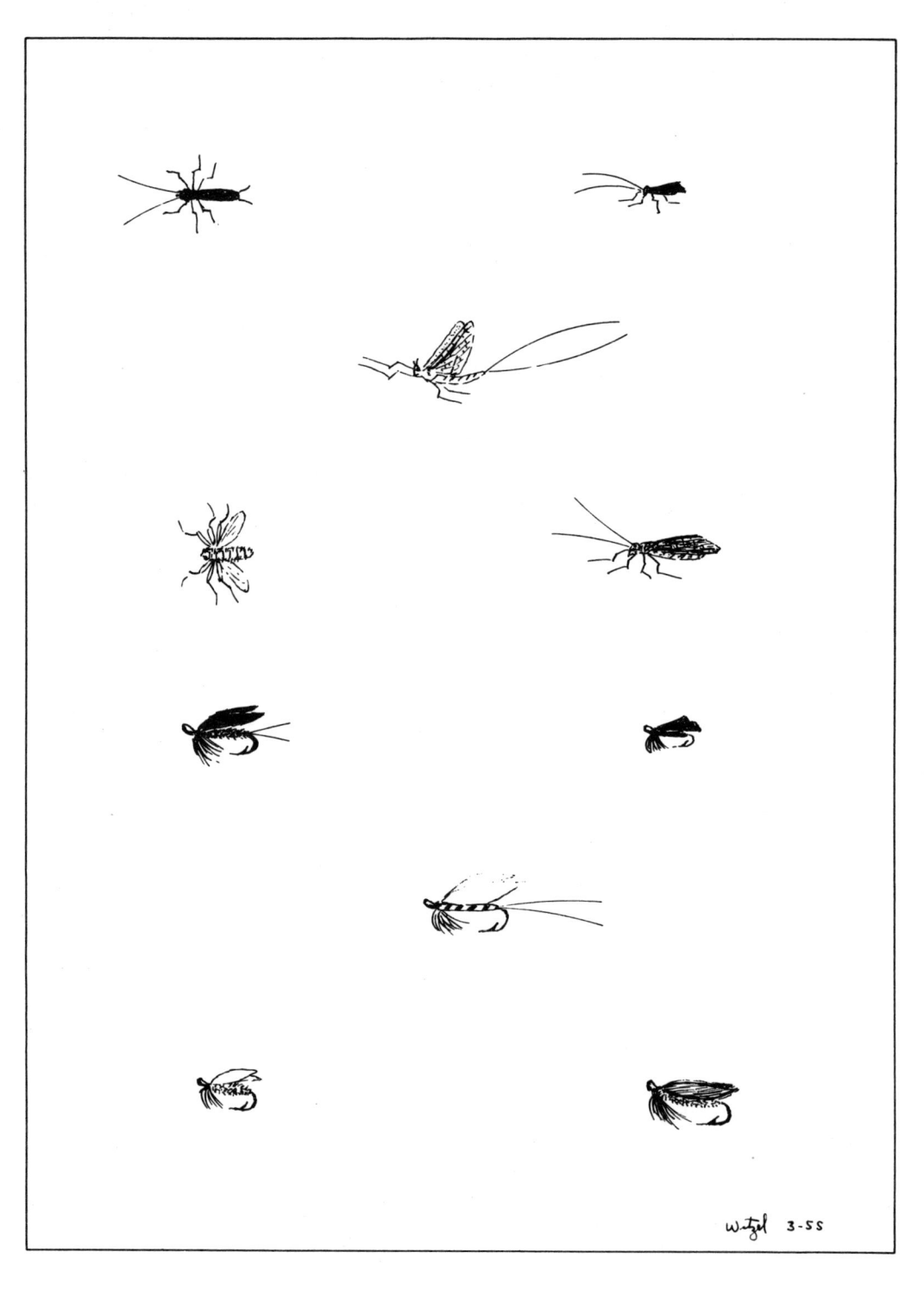

Little Black Stone Fly   Little Black Caddis
Red Quill Spinner
Red Legged March Fly   Alder Fly

The Catalog 49

Trichoptera, this fly is abroad in good numbers on warm sunshiny days and sporadically appears up until the end of May.

IMITATION: Hook, No. 18; wings, coot; body, black wool dubbing; hackle, brown.

* * * *

RED QUILL SPINNER (male imago)

Order—*Ephemeroptera* Genus—*Iron*
Family—*Heptageniidae* Species—*pleuralis*

DESCRIPTION: Length of wings, 3/8 to 7/16 of an inch. General color, reddish brown; wings, glassy; abdomen, reddish brown—tergites and sternites of practically the same color; legs, pale reddish brown with a prominent black spot on each femur; tails, deep red brown.

REMARKS: This is one of the earliest Mayflies to appear and it usually arrives at the time when the snow water is running off. It is in season from the middle of April until the first week in May, but it is sometimes noticed a little later depending on the weather. It is typically a cold water fly and is usually seen in the bright sunshine, rising and falling over the water. This fly is considered by some to be the Gordon Quill; however, it is difficult to reconcile the reddish brown legs with the blue dun hackle used in the imitation fly. The insect illustrated is the male fly in the imago stage; the female is somewhat larger and she is conspicuous by the yellow egg sack at the tip of her abdomen. The fly usually appears over the water during the heat of midday; in fact, most of the hatches occur at this time rather than late evenings, as is customary later on in the season. I have found the fly most successful when tied and fished wet.

IMITATION: Male Red Quill: Hook, No. 12; wings, mallard or starling; body, peacock quill dyed red; hackle, dark red brown, commonly known as red; tail, dark brown feather fibres.

IMITATION: Female Red Quill: Hook, No. 10; wings, mallard; body, peacock quill dyed red, and with a yellow chenille egg sack at the tip; hackle, dark red brown, commonly known as red; tail, dark brown feather fibres.

* * * *

RED LEGGED MARCH FLY

Order—*Diptera* Genus—*Bibio*
Family—*Bibionidae* Species—*femoratus*

DESCRIPTION: Length of wings, 5/16 to 3/8 of an inch. General color blackish; wings, light black; abdomen, black and clothed with whitish hair on the sides; legs, femur blood red, tibia and tarsi, jet black.

REMARKS: The name of the March Fly is rather misleading, for this insect appears over the water during the latter part of April. The pupa stage is apparently passed in the undercut banks of streams, for in such places I have often noticed the flies crawling out of small holes located about a foot above the water. The dressing of the imitation given below has proved most successful, and I have examined trout that were literally gorged on *Bibio femoratus*. The imitation is a favorite with my friend Warren Jones, who keeps it on his leader throughout the season. Along quiet waters or in eddies it is a common sight to see these flies struggling on the water trying to reach land, and if there is one insect that will cause trout to become surface conscious and start taking the dry fly, the Red Legged March Fly is it.

IMITATION: Hook, No. 16, short shank; wings, coot; body, peacock herl; hackle, red furnace—sometimes known as coch-y-bondhu. Instead of the above hackle, I frequently use a combination of jet black and scarlet.

* * * *

ALDER FLY

Order—*Megaloptera* Genus—*Sialis*
Family—*Sialidae* Species—*infumata*

DESCRIPTION: Length to tip of wings, 3/8 to 1/2 an inch. Wings, pale brownish black; abdomen, brownish black; legs, blackish brown; antennae, black.

REMARKS: This fly has a wide distribution and is commonly observed on the underside of bridges, where the females congregate to lay their eggs. These eggs resemble patches of white paint. They usually select such locations so that the eggs when hatched fall directly down into the water. Although the insect is seldom on the surface, except possibly when blown there on windy days, it will always remain a favorite with trout fishermen.

IMITATION: Hook, No. 12; wings, crow; body, peacock herl; hackle, black.

* * * *

BLACK MIDGE

Order—*Diptera* Genus—*Chironomus*
Family—*Chironomidae* Species—*lobiferus*

DESCRIPTION: Length 1/4 to 5/16 of an inch. Wings, greyish white; antennae, dark brown; abdomen, black; legs, yellowish brown.

REMARKS: This fly resembles a mosquito but it does not bite. It is commonly found on slow moving streams and shallow lakes, where it usually appears in great numbers. At night I have seen them so plentiful that the globe of our camp lantern was coated with a thick scum. It appears sporadically throughout the season, from May until September. When it is over the water, the imitation described below will prove very successful. The larvae

PLATE XIV.

Black Midge   Light Stonefly

Black Quill Dun

Early Brown Spinner   Yellow Spider

of these midges live in gelatinous tubes attached to stones on the stream bed, and due to their bright red color are known as Blood Worms.

IMITATION: Hook, No. 16 or 18; wings, starling; body, peacock quill dyed black or black moosemane; hackle, ginger.

* * * *

LIGHT STONE FLY

Order—*Plecoptera* Genus—*Isoperla*
Family—*Perlidae* Species—*signata*

DESCRIPTION: Length to tip of wings, 1/2 to 5/8 of an inch. General color, dark brown; wings, greenish yellow with conspicuous black veins; abdomen, yellow and flushed with pink on the sternites; legs, brown; tails, brown.

REMARKS: The nymph of this fly emerges from the water about the first of May, and the cast off nymphal skins are a common sight on bridge abutments and on rocks protruding above the water. The fly is in season only about a week, and favors those stretches in a stream where the water flows swiftly over a rocky bottom.

IMITATION: Hook, No. 12; wings, mandarin duck or wood duck tied in flat; body, dubbing of yellow and pink wool; hackle, brown; tails, short brown hackle fibres.

* * * *

BLACK QUILL DUN (female imago)

Order—*Ephemeroptera* Genus—*Blasturus*
Family—*Baetidae* Species—*cupidus*

DESCRIPTION: Length of wings, 3/8 to 7/16 of an inch. General color, black; wings, dark bluish grey; abdomen, deep black brown conspicuously ringed; legs, brownish black; tails, fine greyish black and ringed with brown bands.

REMARKS: This fly, also known as the Blue Quill, may be noticed over the slower moving streams from the latter part of April up to the middle of June. On Penns Creek in Pennsylvania, where I now live, it is very common and is generally known as the Black Quill. It exists for two days in this stage; then it sheds the sub-imago skin and ventures forth as the Early Brown Spinner.

IMITATION: Hook, No. 14; wings, dark coot; body, peacock quill dyed bluish black; hackle, dark blackish brown; tails, mandarin duck flank feather.

The Catalog

EARLY BROWN SPINNER (female imago)

Order—*Ephemeroptera* Genus—*Blasturus*
Family—*Baetidae* Species—*cupidus*

DESCRIPTION: Length of wings, 1/2 an inch. General color, blackish brown; wings, dark glassy, stained with reddish brown near the tip; abdomen, tergites dark red brown, sternites somewhat lighter; legs, brown; tails, yellowish, the middle one very short—and all conspicuously ringed with brownish bands.

REMARKS: This fly is the spinner or imago stage of the Black Quill. After the sub-imago skin is shed, the wings lose their slate grey color; and the two outer tails increase in length, the middle one, however, remaining short. This insect is usually found on the slower moving streams and is more or less in season up until the middle of June.

IMITATION: Hook, No. 12; wings, mallard quill feathers; body, brown crewel wool; hackle, dark red brown, commonly known as red; tails, mandarin fibres.

* * * *

YELLOW SPIDER

Order—*Diptera* Genus—*Antocha*
Family—*Tipulidae* Species—*saxicola*

DESCRIPTION: Length of wings, 3/16 to 1/4 of an inch. Wings, glassy, sometimes faintly touched with yellow; body, yellow—some species yellowish brown; legs, yellowish.

REMARKS: This fly favors the slower moving streams and is especially noticeable on cold rainy days. It is a great fly on Pennsylvania's Fishermen's Paradise, Spring Creek. It emerges as early as May 20th, and continues in season until early June. Observations made over the years lead me to believe that this fly appears in greater numbers than any of the other of the crane flies, and autopsies made on many trout reveal an unusually great number of these small crane flies. At times trout feed on them to the exclusion of all others, and on such occasions—as well as through the season—the imitation described below has proved most successful.

IMITATION: Hook, No. 14, short shank; wings, whitish yellow hackle tips; body, yellow crewel wool; hackle, light ginger with extra long fibres.

PLATE XV.

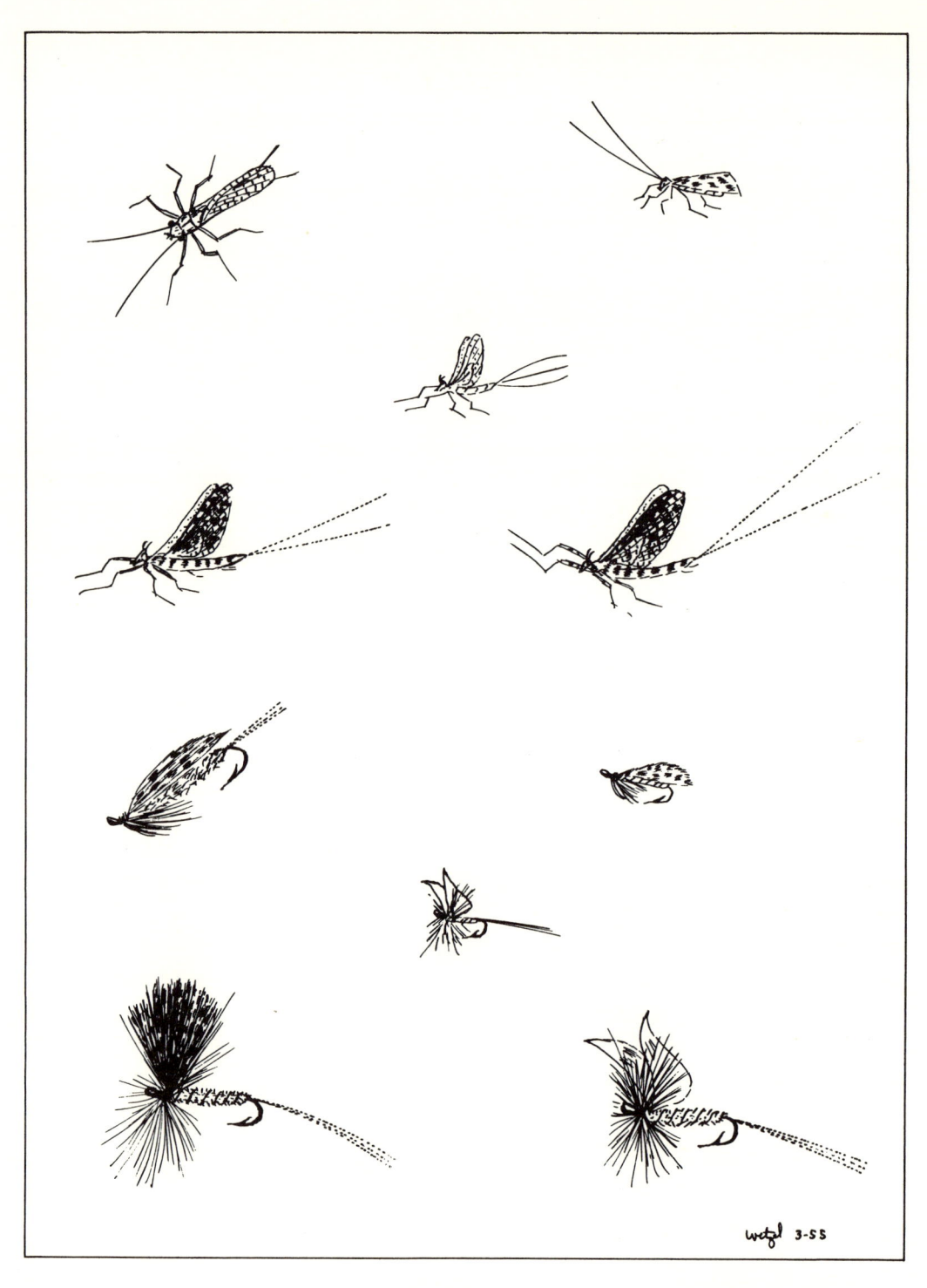

Stone fly

Pale Evening Dun

Spotted Sedge

March Brown

Great Red Spinner

The Catalog

STONE FLY

Order—*Plecoptera* Genus—*Perla*
Family—*Perlidae* Species—*capitata*

DESCRIPTION: Length to tip of wings, 5/8 to 7/8 of an inch. Wings, yellowish brown; body, yellowish brown, the last segment yellow; eyes, black and conspicuously ringed with bright yellow; legs, black with yellowish streaks on sides; tails, brown; antennae, blackish brown.

REMARKS: This fly may be seen sitting quietly on the underside of leaves bordering the stream. When flying over the water it is easily captured, but when approaching it on the shore line it dodges down among the rocks with surprising agility. It favors those stretches in a stream where the water flows swiftly over a rocky bottom, and on the riffles its imitation will be found most successful when fished wet.

IMITATION: Hook, No. 10 long shank; wings, quill feathers from the wings of an English hen pheasant; body, hare's ear dubbing mixed with yellow worsted; hackle, ginger; tails, brown mottled partridge fibres (English).

* * * *

SPOTTED SEDGE

Order—*Trichoptera* Genus—*Hydropsyche*
Family—*Hydropsychidae* Species—*slossonae or alternans*

DESCRIPTION: Length of wings, 5/16 to 7/16 of an inch. Wings, brown and spotted with yellow; body, yellowish brown; legs, golden yellow.

REMARKS: This fly has a wide distribution and is commonly found on rocky, swift water streams. Its larva is the familiar green caddis worm, which fastens its hut, usually made out of debris, on the underside of rocks on the stream bed. The Spotted Sedge appears over the water throughout June, usually at twilight, when the trout are surface feeding. Its imitation has accounted for many large fish.

IMITATION: Hook, No. 16; wings, grouse; body, yellowish brown floss silk, ribbed with fine gold wire; hackle, pale ginger.

* * * *

PALE EVENING DUN (male sub-imago)

Order—*Ephemeroptera* Genus—*Ephemerella*
Family—*Baetidae* Species—*dorothea*

DESCRIPTION: Length of wings, 1/4 to 3/8 of an inch. Wings, grey; abdomen, yellowish orange; legs, yellowish grey; tails, grey.

REMARKS: This fly usually appears when the Black Quill is on the water—sometimes a little later. It is in season from the middle of May up into the second week of June, a period when dry fly fishing is at its peak. It is a great fly on the limestone streams of central Pennsylvania. The artificial fly will be found most successful when these insects are emerging from the water, since they seldom reappear again until after the sub-imago skin is shed.

IMITATION: Hook, No. 14; wings, starling; body, yellow floss silk ribbed with fine gold wire; hackle, dun; tail, dun hackle fibres.

* * * *

MARCH BROWN (male sub-imago)

Order—*Ephemeroptera* Genus—*Stenonema*
Family—*Heptageniidae* Species—*vicarium*

DESCRIPTION: General color, brown; length of wings, 1/2 to 5/8 of an inch. Wings, smoky brown, having black heavy veins creating a mottled appearance; abdomen, yellowish, ringed with dark brown—sternites, light yellowish brown; legs, yellowish brown with black bands on femur and at tibia joint; tails, brown with dark joinings.

REMARKS: This fly comes from a nymph that is found under stones in the swift water. On cold rainy days the March Brown may be noticed clinging to bushes bordering the stream, but its life in this stage is very short. Later in the day, it casts the sub-imago skin and reappears over the water as the Great Red Spinner.

IMITATION: Hook, No. 10; wings, dark mandarin duck rolled; body, dubbing of fur from an English hare's ear, with yellow tying silk; hackle, ginger; tails, brown mandarin fibres.

* * * *

GREAT RED SPINNER (male imago)

Order—*Ephemeroptera* Genus—*Stenonema*
Family—*Heptageniidae* Species—*vicarium*

DESCRIPTION: Length of wings, 1/2 to 5/8 of an inch. Wings, glassy with the front border pale brown near the tip; abdomen, light brown, ringed with deep reddish brown; legs, brown with deep reddish band on the femur and at joint of tibia; tails, olive brown with joinings of a deeper hue.

REMARKS: This fly is the spinner of the March Brown. It lives about three days in this stage and may be seen at dusk rising and falling over the swift water riffles. Its imitation is a most successful fly and good sport may be had with it throughout the season.

IMITATION: Hook, No. 10; wings, mallard; body, hare's ear dubbing with yellow tying silk; hackle, dark ginger; tails, brown mandarin fibres.

The Catalog

GREEN CADDIS

Order—*Trichoptera* Genus—*Rhyacophila*
Family—*Rhyacophilidae* Species—*lobifera*

DESCRIPTION: Length to tip of wings, 7/16 to 9/16 of an inch. Wings varying from a pale brown to a light black; abdomen, bright green; legs, greenish yellow; antennae, light brown.

REMARKS: This fly may be noticed in great numbers congregated on rocks which protrude above swift flowing water. Here and there the Green Caddis may be seen venturing and hesitating near the edge; then as if finally making up their minds they descend beneath the surface to lay their eggs. I have had them fasten their green egg sacks to the submerged portion of my waders while wading in swift water; these eggs are fastened with a glue-like substance and are difficult to remove. Now and then the flies would congregate in a ball about one inch in diameter, rise to the surface, then float down stream, when the ball would break up. Due to its habit of swimming underneath the water, its imitation should be fished wet; in fact, who knows but what long ago this peculiarity may have been the origin of wet fly fishing.

IMITATION: Hook, No. 14; wings, coot; body, green crewel wool, ribbed with gold wire and with a green egg sack near the tip; hackle, ginger dyed a pale greenish yellow.

* * * *

DARK GREEN DRAKE (male sub-imago)

Order—*Ephemeroptera* Genus—*Hexagenia*
Family—*Ephemeridae* Species—*recurvata*

DESCRIPTION: Length of wings, 5/8 to 3/4 of an inch. Wings, dark olive green mottled with brown; abdomen, tergites yellowish brown, sternites somewhat lighter; legs, yellowish brown; tails, brown.

REMARKS: On Penns Creek in Pennsylvania this fly is known as the Dark Green Drake. It appears about the same time as the Green Drake and resembles it somewhat, only its wings are of a deeper greenish brown; it may also be distinguished by its two tails, whereas the Green Drake has three. It is commonly found on brushy mountain streams and may be noticed resting on stones near the water's edge. It exists for two days in this stage; then it casts the sub-imago skin and appears as the Brown Drake.

IMITATION: Hook, No. 8; wings, teal stained a greenish brown; body, brown raffia grass ribbed with fine gold wire; hackle, dark ginger; tails, mandarin fibres.

PLATE XVI.

Green Caddis   Dark Green Drake

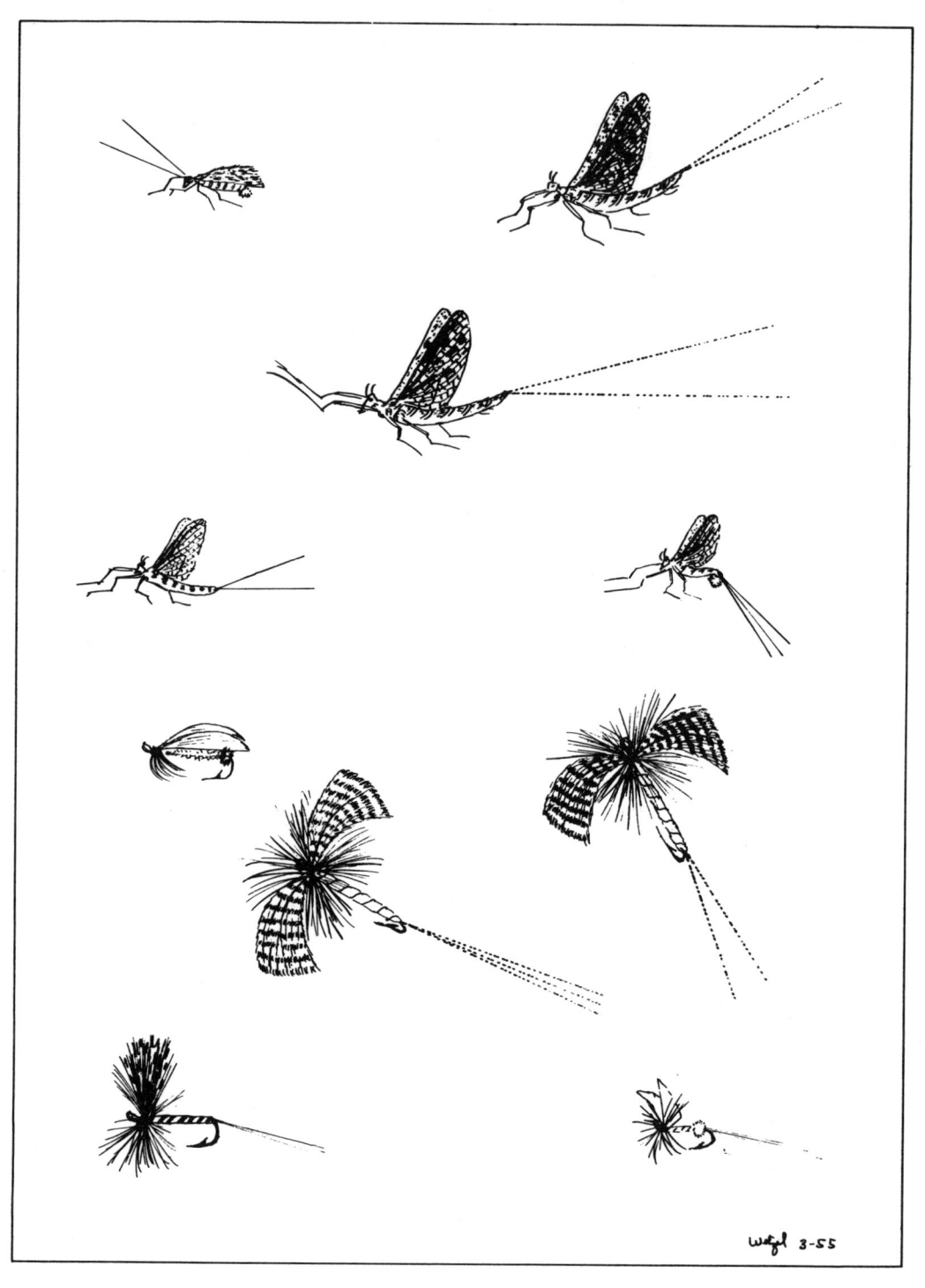

Brown Drake

Ginger Quill Dun   Pale Evening Spinner

The Catalog

BROWN DRAKE (male imago)

Order—*Ephemeroptera* Genus—*Hexagenia*
Family—*Ephemeridae* Species—*recurvata*

DESCRIPTION: Length of wings, 5/8 to 3/4 of an inch. Wings, rich red brown with veins of a deeper brown, giving it a mottled effect; abdomen, tergites rich red brown with yellow joinings at segments, sternites slightly lighter brown; legs, brown; tails, brown about one and three-quarter inches long with dark brown joinings.

REMARKS: When once seen, this fly cannot be forgotten, for its wings are of a sparkling, rich red brown. It is the spinner or imago of the Dark Green Drake, but one would hardly recognize it; its front feet and tail have almost doubled in length and its color has changed to an entirely different hue. Trout simply go wild when the large drakes are on the water, and it is a matter of regret to all fly fishers that the season is so short. This fly resembles *Ephemera simulans* to a marked degree but it is quite a bit larger.

IMITATION: Hook, No. 8, wings, mallard breast feathers stained a rich red brown; body, brown raffia grass ribbed with fine gold wire; hackle, red brown, commonly known as red; tails, mallard stained brown.

* * * *

GINGER QUILL DUN (female sub-imago)

Order—*Ephemeroptera* Genus—*Stenonema*
Family—*Heptageniidae* Species—*fuscum*

DESCRIPTION: Length of wings, 7/16 to 9/16 of an inch. Wings, greyish brown with rather heavy brownish black veins; body, amber; legs, light amber; tails, amber.

REMARKS: This fly resembles the March Brown, except that it is somewhat smaller and its wings are not so heavily clouded. It comes from a nymph found under stones in the swift riffles and lives two days in this stage, sitting quietly on bushes bordering the stream. The artificial can be recommended as being a good all-around fly, but it will be found most successful when its prototype is emerging from the water.

IMITATION: Hook, No. 12; wings, rolled mandarin feather; body, peacock quill; tails, ginger hackle fibres; hackle, ginger.

* * * *

PALE EVENING SPINNER (female imago)

Order—*Ephemeroptera* Genus—*Ephemerella*
Family—*Baetidae* Species—*dorothea*

DESCRIPTION: Length of wings, 3/8 to 7/16 of an inch. Wings, clear and glassy; abdomen, pale yellowish; legs, pale yellowish; tails, white.

REMARKS: This fly, carrying a mass of yellowish eggs at the tip of her abdomen, may be noticed in a compact cloud over the riffles, usually about sundown. I have opened trout whose stomachs were literally gorged with this insect. On some waters, like Penns Creek, it is extremely abundant, and it seems to appear in greatest numbers on dark cloudy days.

IMITATION: Hook, No. 14; wings, starling; body, pale yellow floss silk, ribbed with fine gold wire and tipped with yellow chenille to represent the egg sack; hackle, pale yellow; tails, white hackle fibres.

* * * *

HOUSE FLY

Order—*Diptera*　　　　　　　　Genus—*Musca*
Family—*Muscinae*　　　　　　　Species—*domestica*

DESCRIPTION: Length of wings, 1/4 of an inch; body, black; legs, black.

REMARKS: The imitation described below can be attributed to the Harrisburg Fly Fishers, who rate it one of their best hot weather flies on the flat stretches of such limestone streams as the Letort and Big Spring.

IMITATION: Hook No. 18, short shank; wings, starling tied to conform with natural; body, black spun fur dubbing; hackle, black; head, orange tying silk.

* * * *

GINGER QUILL SPINNER (male imago)

Order—*Ephemeroptera*　　　　　Genus—*Stenonema*
Family—*Heptageniidae*　　　　　Species—*fuscum*

DESCRIPTION: Length of wings, 3/8 to 7/16 of an inch. Wings, glassy with amber or pale reddish in front near the tip; abdomen, thorax, and sternites amber, tergites amber and ringed with reddish brown; legs, ginger or light amber with dark reddish bands on all femora; tails, smoky amber with narrow, dark brown joinings.

REMARKS: At dusk this Mayfly may be noticed in great numbers cruising back and forth over the riffles, many of them flying along in copula. They appear about the middle of May and are in season for the next two weeks.

IMITATION: Hook, No. 12; wings, starling or mallard quills; body, peacock quill; hackle, ginger; tails, ginger hackle fibres or mandarin duck.

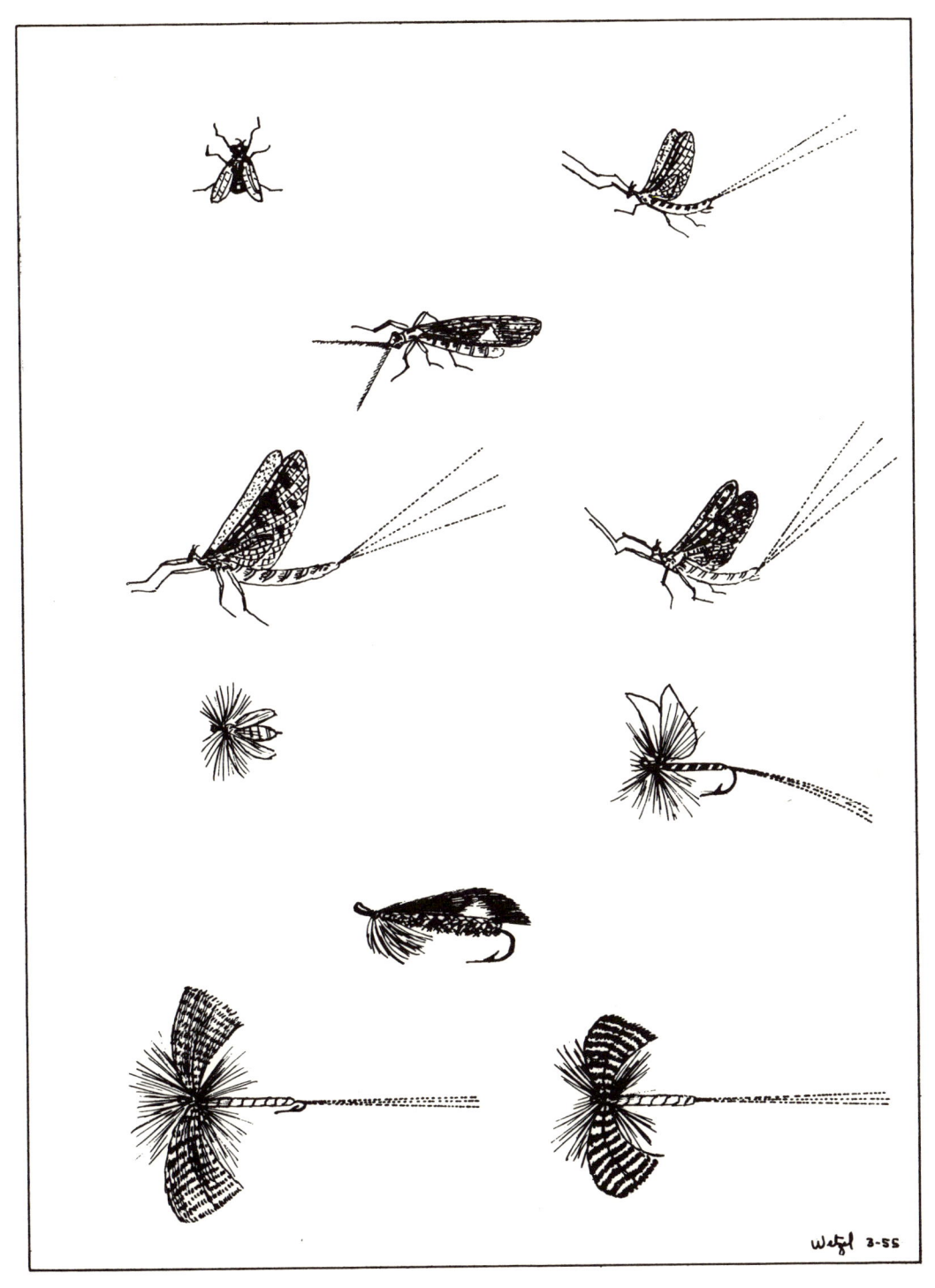

PLATE XVII.

House Fly   Ginger Quill Spinner

           Fish Fly

Green Drake   Black Drake

FISH FLY

Order—*Megaloptera* Genus—*Chauliodes*
Family—*Corydalidae* Species—*serricornis*

DESCRIPTION: Length of wings, 7/8 of an inch. Wings, black and sprinkled with numerous white dots, a white patch in middle of front wing; body, black; legs, greyish brown; antennae, black and sawtoothed.

REMARKS: This fly loves the bright sunshine, and if the weather is propitious it may be noticed in good numbers flying sluggishly here and there among the willows bordering the stream. During the latter part of May and early in June it appears over the water and its imitation is rated as a killing fly on large brown trout. When I originally constructed this pattern it was tied dry, but in more recent years I have changed it over to a wet fly, in which state (no doubt due to its large size) it has proven far more successful.

IMITATION: Hook, No. 6, long shank; wings, turkey quill feathers; body, dubbing of black and brown wool, tied with yellow silk so as to shine through; hackle, dark dun.

* * * *

GREEN DRAKE (female sub-imago)

Order—*Ephemeroptera* Genus—*Ephemera*
Family—*Ephemeridae* Species—*guttulata*

DESCRIPTION: Length of wings, 7/8 to 1 1/16 of an inch. Wings, pale green with conspicuous blackish brown patches; thorax, brown; abdomen, tergites brown with a bright yellow median stripe and sternites yellowish; front legs, femur brown and tibia yellowish; middle and hind legs, yellowish; tails, olive brown with darker joinings.

REMARKS: This fly comes from a whitish transparent nymph which burrows in the stream bed. It emerges from the water as early as May 25th, depending on the temperature, and continues for about three days in the sub-imago stage. In different localities it is known under a variety of names such as Shad Fly, Coffin Fly, Mayfly, and Big Mayfly. On my farm on Penns Creek in Pennsylvania it appears in almost unbelievable numbers. On Spring Creek, at which is located the Fisherman's Paradise, this fly grows to an unusual size, the wings measuring slightly over an inch in length. On dark, cloudy days these flies may be noticed hanging upside down on the underside of blades of grass which protrude above the water, but as soon as the weather grows warm they take wing and rise, higher and higher

The Catalog

until finally they are lost in the tree tops. Nothing more is seen of them until they reappear over the water a few days later, in which state the female is known as the Grey Drake and the male fly as the Black Drake.

IMITATION: Hook, No. 8; wings, mallard flank feather stained green; body, natural raffia grass ribbed with fine gold wire; hackle, pale ginger; tail, fibres from a mandarin feather.

* * * *

BLACK DRAKE (male imago)

Order—*Ephemeroptera* Genus—*Ephemera*
Family—*Ephemeridae* Species—*guttulata*

DESCRIPTION: Length of wings, 1/2 to 5/8 of an inch. Wings, pale yellowish, but so blotched with dark brown as to appear black; thorax, reddish brown; abdomen, pale waxy white; front legs, dark blackish brown; middle and hind legs, yellowish white; tails, brown and conspicuously ringed.

REMARKS: This fly is the metamorphosis of the male Green Drake. Its wings have now lost their green color and appear mainly blackish, whence its name. The older the fly becomes the blacker grow its wings and the whiter the body. It is one of the group called Shad Fly, Mayfly, Big Mayfly, or Coffin fly. It is in season about three days but good sport may be had with its imitation a little longer.

IMITATION: Hook, No. 10; wings, dark teal flank feather stained a pale yellow; body, white raffia grass with fine silver wire ribbing; hackle, light badger; tail, fibres from a mandarin feather.

* * * *

GRANNON*

Order—*Trichoptera* Genus—*Brachycentrus*
Family—*Sericostomatidae* Species—*fuliginosus*

DESCRIPTION: Length to tip of wings, 5/8 of an inch. Wings, rusty brown with some light yellow patches; body, black; antennae, black; legs, blackish brown.

REMARKS: This fly comes from a caddis worm that lives in a square section pyramid case. It transforms into a fly around the latter part of May and appears in great numbers, especially on the larger trout streams and

---

*A similar fly, only smaller, appears over Penns Creek almost continually from April 19 to May 15. My fishing companion, Bill Grant, ties it exactly as described for the Grannon only on a number 14 hook

PLATE XVIII.

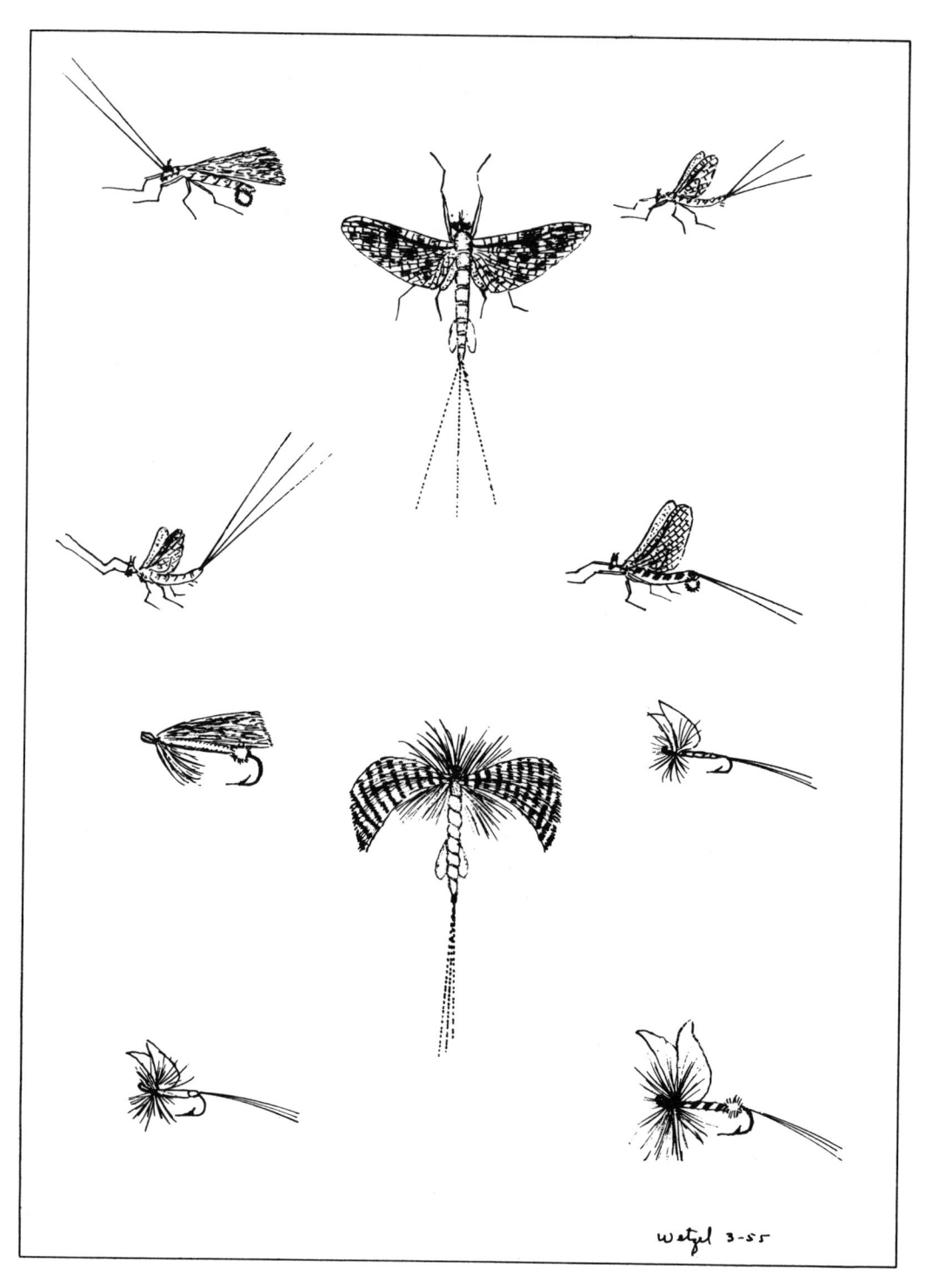

Grannom

Grey Drake

Iron Blue Dun

Jenny Spinner

Brown Quill

The Catalog

rivers. The female is conspicuous by her green egg sack. The wet fly imitation described below can be recommended as an effective fly.

IMITATION; Hook, No. 10; wings, pheasant; body, black floss silk with a green chenille bulb at the rear to represent the egg sack; hackle, blackish brown fibres.

* * * *

IRON BLUE DUN (male sub-imago)

Order—*Ephemeroptera*   Genus—*Leptophlebia*
Family—*Baetidae*   Species—*johnsoni*

DESCRIPTION: Length of wings, 5/16 to 3/8 of an inch. Wings, bluish black; abdomen, brownish olive; legs, brownish black; tails, brown.

REMARKS: Around the latter part of May this insect may be seen rising from the swift water and making its unsteady flight towards land. It exists about three days in this stage; then it sheds the sub-imago skin and appears as the Jenny Spinner. I have raised one of them in captivity and had the opportunity of observing its metamorphosis, a most interesting process. Sometimes before this transformation took place the fly changed to a duller color, due to the loosening of the sub-imago skin; the skin between the wings split open and the Mayfly pulled its thorax and head out of the old case; after its wings and body were freed it flipped backwards upside down, and then while struggling to regain an upright position it pulled out its tails and emerged as a fully developed Jenny Spinner. His wings were now clear and glassy, his front feet and tails had greatly increased in length, and his color had now changed to an entirely different hue.

IMITATION: Hook, No. 16; wings, coot; body, peacock or condor quill dyed olive brown; hackle, dark blue dun; tails, brown hackle fibres.

* * * *

GREY DRAKE (female imago)

Order—*Ephemeroptera*   Genus—*Ephemera*
Family—*Ephemeridae*   Species—*guttulata*

DESCRIPTION: Length of wings, 3/4 to 11/16 of an inch. Wings, very faint greenish yellow, mottled with purplish brown spots; thorax, brown; abdomen, creamy, waxy white with the last segment reddish brown; front legs, brown; middle and hind legs, yellowish white; tails, yellowish with blackish brown joinings.

REMARKS: This fly is the metamorphosis of the female Green Drake and is of great importance to the fly fisher. Her wings have lost their former green tint and are pale yellow, mottled with purplish black spots. This is probably the most important one of the group known as Shad Flies, Mayflies, Coffin Flies, or Big Mayflies, since she is crammed with eggs clear up to her head. She can often be noticed just before dark carrying two cylindrical egg packets near the end of her abdomen. When the fly is well on the water, large trout rise to the top and start feeding ravenously on the surface. It is a scene of great excitement until a few minutes after dark. After that the spent fly can be noticed in large scum-like patches floating down on the current.

IMITATION: Hook, No. 8; wings, mallard flank feather stained pale yellow; body, white raffia grass ribbed with fine silver wire and with two tufts of yellowish white wool underneath to represent the egg sacks; hackle, light badger; tails, fibres from a mandarin feather.

* * * *

JENNY SPINNER (male imago)

Order—*Ephemeroptera*   Genus—*Leptophlebia*
Family—*Baetidae*   Species—*johnsoni*

DESCRIPTION: Length of wings, 5/16 to 3/8 of an inch. Wings, glassy with a brownish front border extending from the tip down to one-third the depth of the wing; head and thorax, reddish brown; abdominal segments two to seven, white and eight to ten, reddish brown; legs, brown; tails, whitish and ringed with reddish brown.

REMARKS: This fly is the metamorphosis of the Iron Blue Dun. It is a dainty insect and probably the most attractive Mayfly the angler will encounter. It appears in good numbers on Pennsylvania's Kettle Creek and the First Fork of the Sinnemahoning. Towards evening the males appear in companies rising and falling in an amorous dance over the water, and at such time the imitation dry fly will prove the most successful.

IMITATION: Hook, No. 16; wings, starling or light mallard quills; body, white floss silk tipped with crimson; hackle, brown; tails, white hackle fibres.

* * * *

BROWN QUILL SPINNER (female imago)

Order—*Ephemeroptera*   Genus—*Siphlonurus*
Family—*Baetidae*   Species—*quebecensis*

DESCRIPTION: Length of wings, 9/16 to 5/8 of an inch. Wings, glassy and long and narrow; thorax, reddish brown; abdomen, prominently ringed—tergites reddish brown, sternites yellowish white; legs, brown; tails, yellowish and ringed with brown.

The Catalog

REMARKS: This fly is best known by the green ball of eggs attached to the tip of her abdomen. It appears over the water about the end of May and at dusk may be noticed flying back and forth over the riffles. The imitation described below can be heartily recommended, for it is one of the best of the quill flies. Perhaps its success can be attributed to the egg sack; in any event, flies so decorated seem to catch more trout than the conventional type.

IMITATION: Hook, No. 12; wings, the lightest of light mallard or white duck quills; body, peacock quill tipped with green chenille to imitate the egg sack; hackle, reddish brown, commonly known as red; tails, mandarin fibres or red hackle tips.

* * * *

ORANGE CRANEFLY

Order—*Diptera*   Genus—*Tipula*
Family—*Tipulidae*   Species—*bicornis*

DESCRIPTION: Length of wings, 7/16 to 9/16 of an inch. Wings, clear and faintly tinted with yellowish orange; body, orange; legs, pale yellowish.

REMARKS: This fly is commonly observed around slow moving waters, especially in damp swampy regions. Its mating flight occurs around twilight, when quite frequently both male and female fall on the water in copula. When skated across the water, the imitation described below has accounted for some large trout.

IMITATION: Hook, No. 10 long shank; wings, pale yellow hackle tips tied on horizontally; body, orange wool; hackle, pale yellow with long fibres such as saddle or spade hackles.

* * * *

WHIRLING CRANE FLY

Order—*Diptera*   Genus—*Tipula*
Family—*Tipulidae*   Species—*bella or furca*

DESCRIPTION: Length of wings, 5/8 to 3/4 of an inch. Wings, grey and black streaked; body, greenish brown; thorax, brown; legs, greenish brown.

REMARKS: This fly comes from a water worm found in the muck along the stream. It is commonly seen clinging to the damp vertical face of stone cliffs rising from the water, and near such places they often swarm in great numbers. Like the Orange Crane fly described above, the imitation will be found most successful when skated across the surface of the water.

IMITATION: Hook, No. 8, long shank; wings, grey hackle tips tied on horizontally or in a spent position; body, olive wool; hackle, olive dun with long fibres, such as a saddle hackle.

* * * *

BLUE BOTTLE

Order—*Diptera*   Genus—*Lucilia*
Family—*Muscidae*   Species—*caesar*

DESCRIPTION: Length of wings, 3/8 to 7/16 of an inch. Wings, glassy; body, greenish blue; eyes, brown; legs, bluish black.

REMARKS: This is the well known blow fly that lays its eggs on meat and dead animals. On windy days it is quite often blown on the water, and its imitation is considered by many a valuable fly.

IMITATION: Hook, No. 12; wings, mallard or starling quills; body, blue floss silk ribbed with black thread; hackle, black.

* * * *

GOLDEN EYED GAUZE WING

Order—*Neuroptera*   Genus—*Chrysopa*
Family—*Chrysopidae*   Species—*occulata*

DESCRIPTION: Length of wings, 1/2 an inch. Wings, pale green; abdomen, pale green; legs, pale green; antennae, pale green.

REMARKS: On windy days this fly is frequently blown on the water and good sport may then be had with its imitation. With its brilliant gold eyes and pretty green color it is a most attractive looking insect, yet it emits a very disagreeable odor.

IMITATION: Hook, No. 12; wings, duck quills stained a pale green; body, pale green floss silk ribbed with thread of the same color; hackle, green (dyed).

* * * *

WHITE MAYFLY (female imago)

Order—*Ephemeroptera*   Genus—*Stenonema*
Family—*Heptageniidae*   Species—*rubromaculatum*

DESCRIPTION: Length of wings, 1/2 to 9/16 of an inch. Wings, glassy with a purplish red amber stain near the front border; abdomen, white with tergites flushed with pale pink; front legs, pale whitish amber; middle and hind legs, alabaster white; tails, whitish with blackish brown joinings.

REMARKS: This is a great fly on Brodheads Creek in Pennsylvania. The female, conspicuous by her pink egg sack, appears over the water about the latter part of June. The male fly is somewhat smaller and his wings are not so deeply amber tinted on the front. While I have no definite

PLATE XIX.

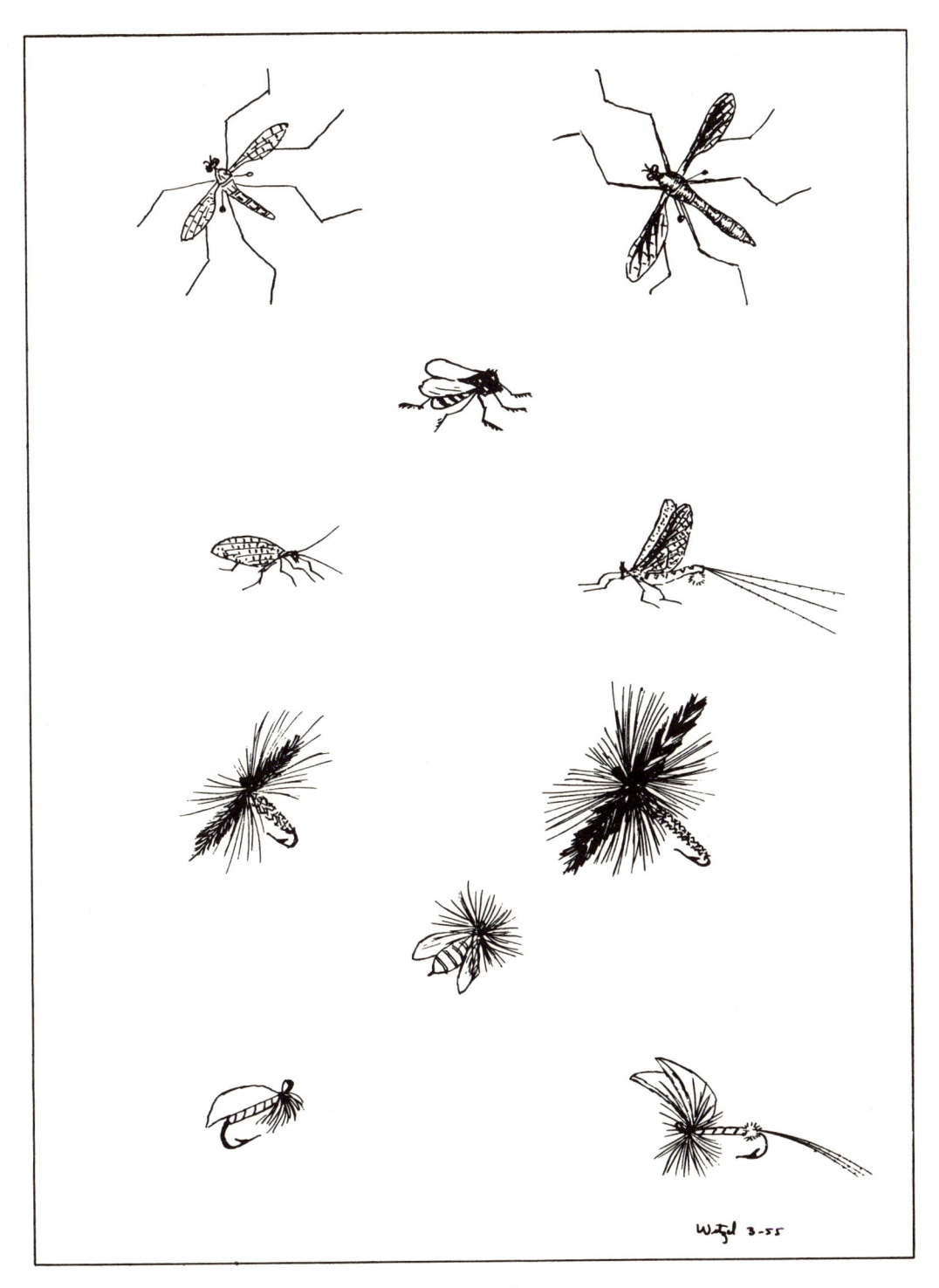

Orange Crane fly   Whirling Crane fly
           Blue Bottle
Golden Eyed Gauze Wing   White Mayfly

proof, I believe that the sub-imago stage of this fly has pink wings, for I have seen such flies over the water a day or two before the White Mayfly made its appearance.

IMITATION: Hook, No. 10; wings, white duck quills married with pink on the front; body, white floss silk, ribbed with pink thread and having a pink chenille bulb near the end to represent the egg sack; hackle, white; tails, fibres from a grey mallard flank feather.

* * * *

WHITE GLOVED HOWDY (female imago)

Order—*Ephemeroptera*   Genus—*Isonychia*
Family—*Baetidae*   Species—*albomanicata*

DESCRIPTION: Length of wings, 9/16 to 5/8 of an inch. Wings, glassy; abdomen, reddish brown; front legs, brown with white tarsi; middle and hind legs, yellowish white; tails, white and reddish brown at base.

REMARKS: About the end of June this fly may be seen flying back and forth over the riffles, especially at dusk on the mountain streams. It is a great fly on Pennsylvania's Kettle Creek. The male apparently flies after dark, for he is seldom seen over the water. The first artificial I ever tied was a rather bungling attempt to imitate this insect. I have taken many trout on it and have changed its dressing very little since that day years ago in the Kettle Creek country. The natural insect is prominent by its white front feet; when these are extended at rest it gives the impression as if ready to shake hands, and for that reason Dr. J. G. Needham has aptly named it the White Gloved Howdy.

IMITATION: Hook, No. 12; wings, mallard quill feathers; body, reddish brown wool; hackle, badger with brown center; tails, white fibres from the base of a Lady Amherst tippet.

* * * *

YELLOW SALLY

Order—*Plecoptera*   Genus—*Isoperla*
Family—*Perlidae*   Species—*bilineata*

DESCRIPTION: Length to tip of wings, 3/8 to 1/2 an inch. Wings, greenish yellow; abdomen, yellow; legs, yellow; tails, yellowish brown; antennae, yellowish brown.

REMARKS: At dusk this stone fly may be noticed in great abundance flying back and forth over the riffles. It appears rather late in the season and is commonly observed throughout the month of July. Among the family, yellow and green predominate. Usually when *Isoperla bilineata* is over

PLATE XX.

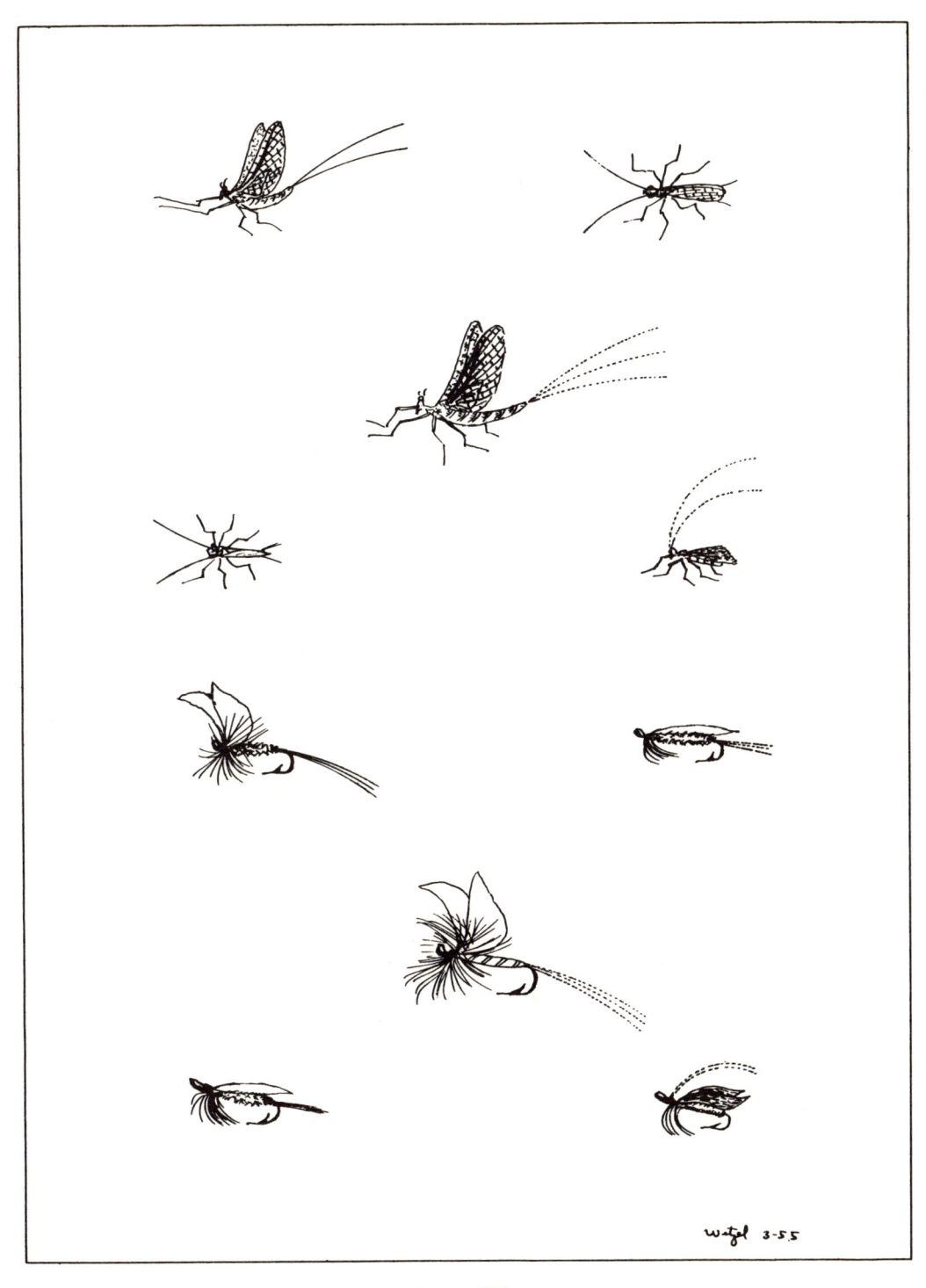

White Gloved Howdy   Yellow Sally
                  Golden Spinner
Willow or Needle Fly   Brown Silverhorns

the water it is accompanied by a smaller, bright green species, *Alloperla imbecilla;* and on such occasions the fly fisher would do well to have imitations of both species readily available.

IMITATION—Yellow Sally: Hook, No. 14; wings, duck quills stained a pale yellow; body, dubbing of yellow fur; hackle, pale ginger; tails, mandarin fibres.

IMITATION: Green Stone fly: Hook, No. 16; wings, duck quills stained a light green; body, green floss silk; hackle, light green; tails, light green.

* * * *

GOLDEN SPINNER (female imago)

Order—*Ephemeroptera* Genus—*Potamanthus*
Family—*Ephemeridae* Species—*distinctus*

DESCRIPTION: Length of wings, 5/8 of an inch. Wings, golden yellow; abdomen, pale yellowish; pronotum with a red dorsal stripe; front legs, femur and tibia red, tarsus yellow; middle and hind legs, yellow; tails, yellowish white with reddish brown joinings.

REMARKS: On warm evenings this fly may be noticed over the water, but it is most active from nightfall until early mornings. The male is about three-fourths as large as the female, and his wings are clear and transparent except near the front border, where traces of golden yellow exist. This fly is usually found in large, fast flowing streams and may be noticed emerging from the quieter eddies—the place where the nymph spends its life burrowing in the silt and trash.

IMITATION: Hook, No. 10; wings, duck quills dyed a golden yellow; body, golden yellow Plastacele or natural raffia grass; hackle, yellow; tails, mandarin fibres.

* * * *

WILLOW OR NEEDLE FLY

Order—*Plecoptera* Genus—*Leuctra*
Family—*Nemouridae* Species—*grandis*

DESCRIPTION: Length to tip of wings, 3/8 to 7/16 of an inch. Wings, pale reddish brown; body, greyish brown; legs, brown; tails, brown, antennae, brown.

REMARKS: I have seldom encountered the Needle Fly in any great abundance, yet it is eagerly taken by trout. Its rather long wings are rolled at rest, which gives it a needle-like appearance, whence its name. It may be noticed flying low over the stony riffles, and in such places its imitation will be found most successful.

IMITATION: Hook, No. 14; wings, brown mallard; body, dubbing of mole's fur; hackle, brown; tails, brown hackle fibres.

The Catalog

BROWN SILVERHORNS

Order—*Trichoptera* Genus—*Athripsodes*
Family—*Leptocerinae* Species—*wetzeli*

DESCRIPTION: Length to tip of wings, 3/8 of an inch. Wings, dark brown; body, dark brown; antennae, brown with narrow white rings along the entire length.

REMARKS: Mr. H. H. Ross, Systematic Entomologist of the Illinois Natural History Survey Division, honored the present writer by naming this caddis fly after him. It appears in great numbers on Kettle Creek around the end of June, at which time the artificial is most successful. One of the most conspicuous features of this insect is its white banded antennae, whence its name Silverhorns.

IMITATION: Hook, No. 16; wings, dark brown duck quills (dyed); body, dark brown floss silk; hackle, dark brown commonly known as red; antennae, fibres from a teal tippet.

* * * *

WHITE CADDIS

Order—*Trichoptera* Genus—*Leptocella*
Family—*Leptocerinae* Species—*exquisita*

DESCRIPTION: Length to tip of wings, 7/16 to 1/2 an inch. Wings, white; abdomen, green; legs, yellowish white; antennae, yellowish.

REMARKS: Without much doubt this is the prototype of that old favorite erroneously named the Deer Fly. It is commonly found from Canada to Florida and is over the water from twilight to early morning. Its imitation—wrongly named the Deer Fly—has stood the test of time and will always remain a tried and true favorite.

IMITATION: Hook, No. 12; wings, white duck quills; body, green floss silk; hackle, white.

* * * *

YELLOW DRAKE (female imago)

Order—*Ephemeroptera* Genus—*Ephemera*
Family—*Ephemeridae* Species—*varia*

DESCRIPTION: Length of wings, 5/8 to 11/16 of an inch. Wings, pale yellowish with a few small brownish patches; thorax, yellowish brown; abdominal tergites, yellowish white with black streaks; sternites, creamy white; front legs, femur and tibia brownish; middle and hind legs, creamy white; tails, yellowish and ringed with dark brown joinings.

REMARKS: This insect appears during the early part of July and continues more or less in season for the next two weeks. Just at dark the female insect starts laying her eggs, and at this time she may be noticed flying unusually low over the water. Her favorite place for this performance is over the riffles leading into the slower moving pools, and while so employed she may be seen rising and falling, rarely ascending more than a foot or so above the water; on her descent she rides the current for a short distance downstream, and it is at this time, when voiding her eggs, that she is eagerly preyed upon by trout.

IMITATION: Hook, No. 10; wings, mallard quills stained a pale yellow; body, yellow Plastacele or natural raffia grass; hackle, badger; tails, mandarin fibres.

* * * *

BIG ORANGE SEDGE

Order—*Trichoptera* Genus—*Neuronia*
Family—*Phryganeidae* Species—*postica*

DESCRIPTION: Length to tip of wings, 1 to 1 1/8 of an inch. Wings, orange, sprinkled with a few brownish spots near the front border; body, yellowish brown; legs, yellow; antennae, reddish and banded with black rings.

REMARKS: This fly appears in good numbers on lakes and on the streams flowing into them. When once seen it cannot be forgotten, for its wings are brilliant orange and quite conspicuous. It appears mainly after dark but in early mornings it may still be seen flying above the water. The imitation can be recommended as an excellent fly when fished wet in the deep heavy riffles.

IMITATION: Hook, No. 8; wings, duck quills dyed orange; body, yellowish brown floss silk, ribbed with brown thread; antennae, teal dyed a reddish brown; hackle, yellow.

* * * *

DEER FLY

Order—*Diptera* Genus—*Chrysops*
Family—*Tabanidae* Species—*vittatus*

DESCRIPTION: Length to tip of wings, 1/4 to 5/16 of an inch. Wings, glassy and spotted with brown; eyes, bright gold; thorax, blackish brown; abdomen, tan—the end segments blackish brown; legs, ginger.

REMARKS: This fly, appearing about the end of June, is in season throughout the summer, much to the annoyance of the fly fisher. Only the females bite, and consequently males are not found near animals or man. Both sexes, however, rest on the bushes bordering the stream and dip down

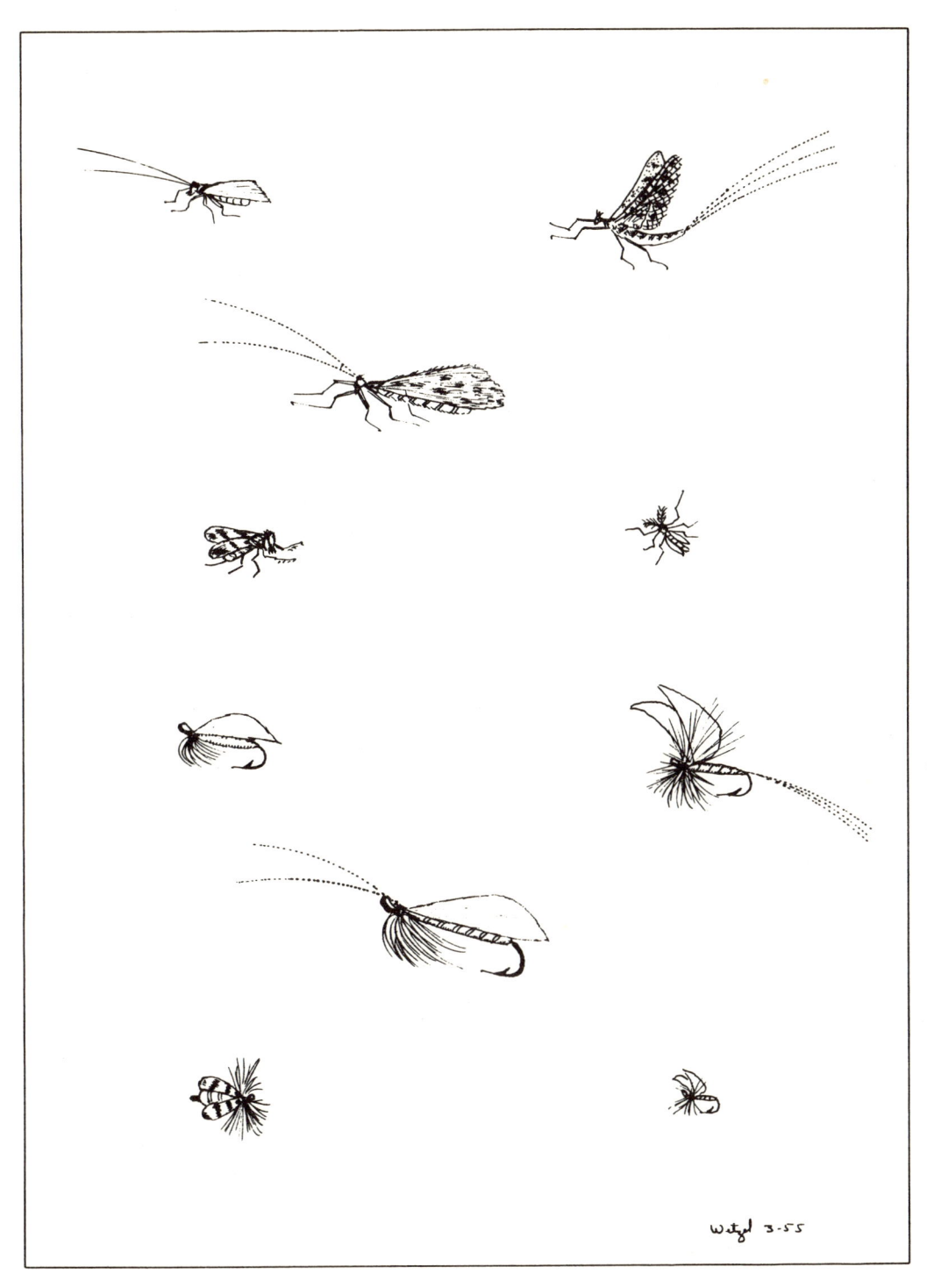

PLATE XXI.

White Caddis Yellow Drake
Big Orange Sedge
Deer Fly Green Midge

into the surface of the water, where they are caught by trout. The imitation of this fly deviates considerably from the well-known deer fly patterns. The green and white artificial, long known as the Deer Fly was incorrectly named and was without doubt patterned after *Leptocella exquisita*, one of the common caddis flies. Mary Orvis Marbury, in her *Favorite Flies*, also questioned the authenticity of its prototype but volunteered no explanation as to its identity, except by saying that: "It is very like one of the little millers or moths we often see in the summertime." When we consider that caddis flies are known as moths in some localities, it is reasonable to presume that she was referring to either *Leptocella exquisita* or *L. albida*.

IMITATION: Hook, No. 14 short shank; wings, brown and white turkey quills; body, tan floss silk, ribbed with black thread and tipped with black; hackle, ginger.

* * * *

GREEN MIDGE (male)

Order—*Diptera* Genus—*Chironomus*
Family—*Chironomidae* Species—*modestus*

DESCRIPTION: Length 1/8 to 3/16 of an inch. Wings, glassy; antennae, brownish; abdomen, bright green; legs, yellowish green.

REMARKS: This fly is found over the water in early May and again in July, when its imitation appears to be the most successful. This can probably be attributed to the fact that small flies are most effective when the streams are low and clear, as in July. The larva is yellow in color and is found in tubes on the stream bed. *Chironomus plumosus*, the Golden Dun Midge described by Ronalds in his *Fly Fisher's Entomology*, is also native to American waters. The angler might find it profitable to have imitations of both species available.

IMITATION—Green Midge: Hook, No. 20; wings, pale starling; body, bright green floss silk, ribbed with fine gold wire; hackle, yellowish green (dyed).

IMITATION—Golden Dun Midge (after Ronalds): Hook, No. 14; wings, pale starling; body, olive floss silk, ribbed with gold twist; hackle, dun.

* * * *

BLACK ANT

Order—*Hymenoptera* Genus—*Camponotus*
Family—*Formicidae* Species—*pennsylvanicus*

DESCRIPTION: Length, 1/2 to 5/8 of an inch. Body, black; legs, black.

REMARKS: This fly was originally designed by my old friend, the late Bob McCafferty. On Brodheads Creek in Pennsylvania it towers head and

The Catalog

shoulders above all others, and is the only fly that consistently takes trout throughout the season. It is highly effective on the limestone waters, particularly in small sizes. This fly cannot be too highly recommended.

IMITATION: Hook, No. 10; build up the body by forming the two bulbs with black tying silk; fasten off, and then cover with two coats of lacquer. When dry, wind on a black hackle at the middle and fasten off in the usual way. The quality and amount of hackle determines whether it is a wet or dry fly, or whether the same fly is fished both ways.

* * * *

SCUD

Order—*Amphipoda* Genus—*Gammarus*
Family—*Gammaridae* Species—*minus*

DESCRIPTION: Length of body, 3/8 to 1/2 an inch. Body and legs, transparent yellowish amber; eyes, black and bright; legs, 14 pair, 8 on thorax, 6 on abdomen—those on thorax the longest.

REMARKS: This fresh water shrimp is found among the roots of water cress, usually in cold swampy streams. On some waters it is extremely abundant, and where so found its imitation proves to be a most killing fly.

IMITATION: Hook, No. 14, the shank bent on a fairly sharp radius; hackle, yellow and tied in Palmer style; body, yellow Plastacele or heavy cellophane wound over hackle, allowing some fibres to project out on the underside; antennae, yellow hackle wisps.

* * * *

LITTLE DAMSEL FLY NYMPH

Order—*Odonata* Genus—*Ischnura*
Family—*Coenagriidae* Species—*verticalis*

DESCRIPTION: Thorax, greenish brown; tails, three, conspicuous and greenish yellow brown in color; legs, greenish yellow brown.

REMARKS: This nymph is quickly recognized by its three flat gill plates, which are carried like tails at the tip of its abdomen. The edges of these tails are set vertically and are swung from side to side while swimming—similar to that of a fish. This nymph favors aquatic vegetation and is commonly found among the pond weed *Potamogeton*.

IMITATION: Hook, No. 12; body, dubbing of dirty greenish yellow brown fur; wing cases, a greenish brown feather bent down near the eye of hook, the fibres then separated to form the legs of the nymph; tails, fine greenish yellow brown hackle tips set in a vertical position.

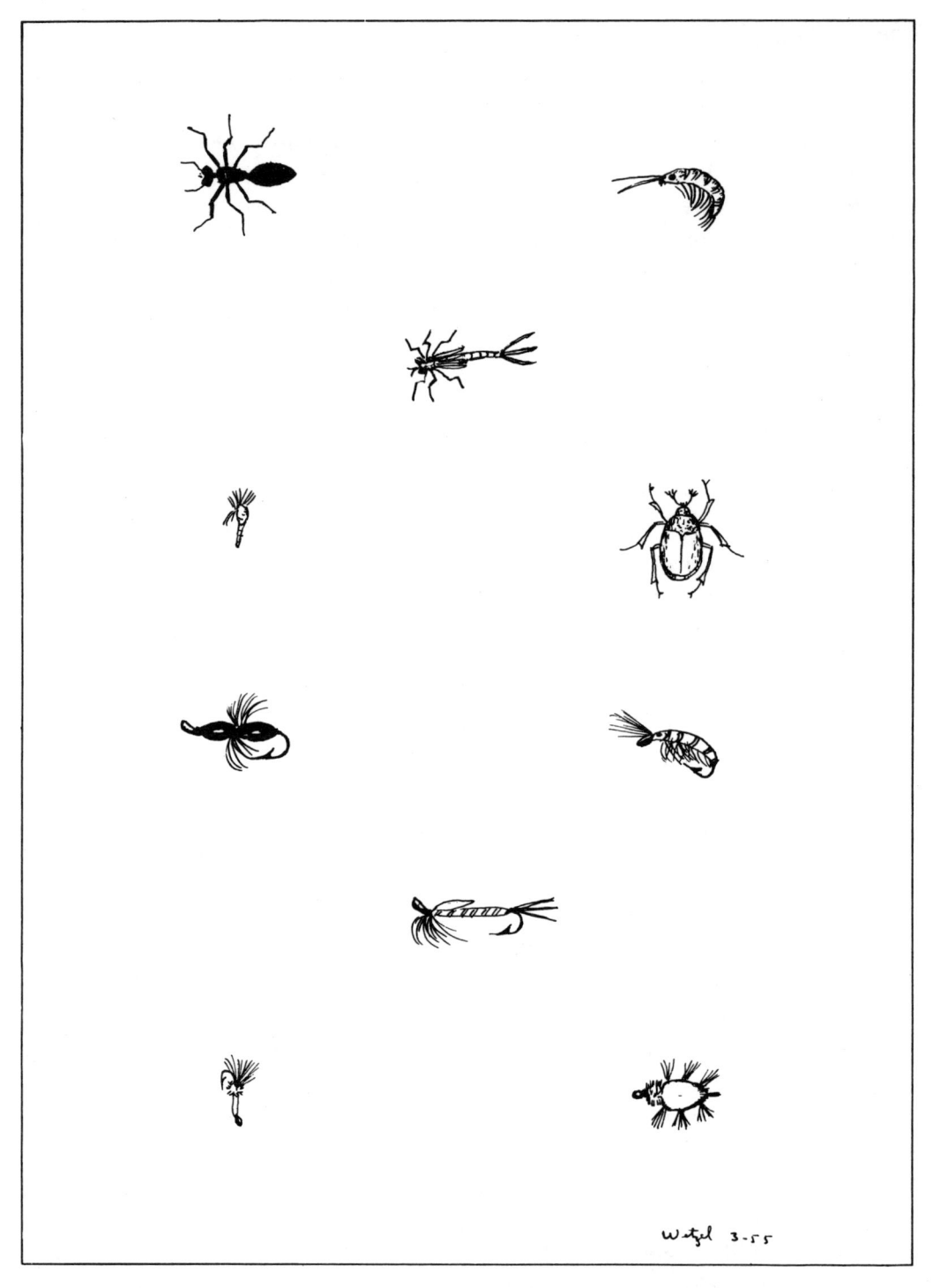

PLATE XXII.

Black Ant
Little Damsel Fly Nymph
Midge Pupa
Scud
Japanese Beetle

The Catalog

MIDGE PUPA

Order—*Diptera*　　　　　　　Genus—*Chironomus*
Family—*Chironomidae*　　　　Species—*modestus*

DESCRIPTION: Length, 3/16 to 1/4 of an inch. General color green; respiratory filaments, white.

REMARKS: The pupal stage of the midge is passed within the larval case on the stream bed, but near the end of the period it rises to the surface and floats vertically for a short time, waiting for its transformation. Among the genus a wide variety of color is found, such as grey, yellow, green, brown, and black. Equip yourself with imitations of these colors, for the Midge Pupa, when fished near the surface, is a most killing fly. It is difficult to sense when a trout takes this fly, for they take it and spit it out with such an imperceptible movement that the angler is hardly ever aware of the rise to the fly. Strike at the turn of the fish, or place a dry fly farther up the leader, which will serve as a float. After one cultivates the time to strike, the number of fish this fly will take is astounding.

IMITATION: Hook, No. 20; body, pale green floss silk, with a green chenille collar; hackle, white—very small and fine. The appearance of this fly deviates considerably from the usual run and a few words on its evolution might prove of interest. The collar of green chenille simulates the enlarged thorax of the pupa with its rapidly developing wings; the hackle in a general way imitates the bristle-like respiratory filaments, and it is wound on near the bend of the hook, a position which will cause the fly to float vertically when using a submerged leader.

* * * *

JAPANESE BEETLE

Order—*Coleoptera*　　　　　Genus—*Popillia*
Family—*Rutelidae*　　　　　Species—*japonica*

DESCRIPTION: Length 7/16 to 1/2 an inch. Head and thorax, shining bronze green; wing covers, tan or brownish and tinged with green on the edges. Along the sides of the abdomen are white spots, and two very distinct white spots are at the tip of the abdomen below the wing covers.

REMARKS: The imitation described below is a slight variation of the pattern designed by Vince Marinaro of the Harrisburg Fly Fishers. They have used it most successfully on the Yellow Breeches, and the Letort, and they rate it as one of the best flies on limestone waters.

IMITATION: Hook, No. 16; body, black tying silk with black hackle Palmer tied; wing cases, two Jungle Cock eyes one on top the other, with the shiny side exposed to view; head, peacock sword feather.

IRON BLUE NYMPH

Order—*Ephemeroptera* Genus—*Leptophlebia*
Family—*Baetidae* Species—*johnsoni*

DESCRIPTION: Thorax, yellowish orange; tergites, yellowish orange; sternites, yellowish; legs, yellowish orange; tails, yellowish brown; gills, small and indistinct.

REMARKS: This nymph lives quite openly in swift flowing water, especially on gravelly riffles. Its body is more or less streamlined, which enables it to maintain its position in the current. One can often see them clinging to stones in the swift shallow water, their heads always upstream and their bodies swaying with the current. Living in such an open and unconcealed environment, they furnish an abundant food supply for trout as they dart from stone to stone. The artificial described below has accounted for many fish, especially in the evenings when the trout desert the deeper pools and venture out in search of food on the gravelly riffles.

IMITATION: Hook, No. 16; body, dubbing of yellowish orange fox fur, enlarged at the thorax; tails, yellowish brown moosemane; wing cases, yellowish orange feather, turned down in front and the projecting fibres separated to form the legs.

* * * *

OLIVE DUN NYMPH

Order—*Ephemeroptera* Genus—*Ephemerella*
Family—*Baetidae* Species—*fuscata*

DESCRIPTION: Thorax, dirty olive brown; tergites, dirty olive brown; sternites, yellowish brown; legs, pale yellow, the femora large, flat and conspicuous; tails, dark brown and very short; gills, indistinct and overlapping each other along the body.

REMARKS: The most conspicuous feature about this nymph is its broad flat and hairy body. It moves about very little on the stream-bed and is commonly found sprawled in the mud and silt, its body usually covered with dirt.

IMITATION: Hook, No. 14; body, brown floss silk, tied loosely and then saturated with lacquer or Duco; when almost dry take pliers and flatten body out to the desired shape of its prototype, meanwhile picking out fibres with the dubbing needle to give it a frowsy appearance; legs, short tufts of yellow wool pressed flat and treated as described above; tails, brown moosemane; wing cases, brown nail from a Jungle Cock feather.

PLATE XXIII.

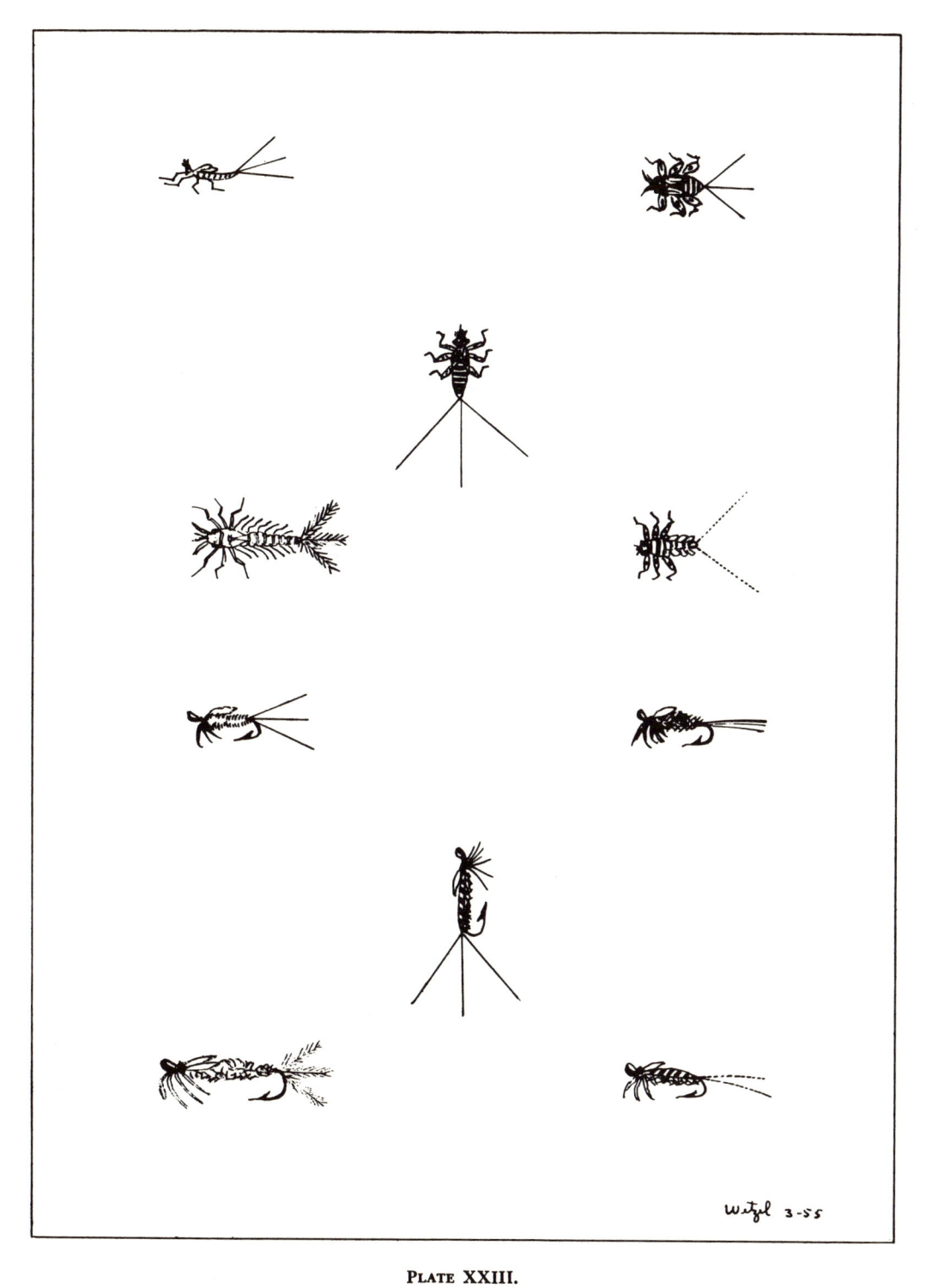

Iron Blue Nymph Ginger Quill Nymph Olive Green Nymph

Green Drake Nymph Red Quill Nymph

GINGER QUILL NYMPH

Order—*Ephemeroptera* Genus—*Stenonema*
Family—*Heptageniidae* Species—*fuscum*

DESCRIPTION: Thorax, brown; tergites, brown and black banded; sternites, yellowish; legs, brown and black banded; tails, brown; gills, small, brown above and yellowish beneath.

REMARKS: This is one of the most common forms of nymphs found on streams having a rocky bottom. Lift up any stone found on the stream-bed, and a number can usually be seen scuttling for some dark crevice. The nymph has a depressed body and its tails are usually apart, as shown in the sketch.

IMITATION: Hook, No. 12; body, first tied loosely with yellow wool, leaving a tuft about an inch long extending out towards the tail, which will later be doubled back on the underside after the fly is ribbed; ribbing, a blend of yellow and brown moosemane, which will give a mottled effect; the whole then saturated with lacquer or Duco and when almost dry pressed flat with pliers; legs, brownish black moosemane; tails, wood duck or mandarin fibres; wing cases, nail from a Jungle Cock feather.

* * * *

GREEN DRAKE NYMPH

Order—*Ephemeroptera* Genus—*Ephemera*
Family—*Ephemeridae* Species—*guttulata*

DESCRIPTION: Thorax, yellowish white; tergites, white; sternites, white; legs, yellowish white; tails, yellowish white and heavily fringed; gills, white and hairy.

REMARKS: This is the nymph of the Shad Fly or Coffin Fly, and it burrows in the mud, sand, and gravel on the stream-bed. How the trout ever find them is questionable, but the fact remains that they feed heavily on them throughout the season—not only at the time when the nymph is emerging to transform into the Green Drakes. I have knocked many a trout over the head that disgorged these nymphs, all of which proves that trout prey on them throughout the season.

IMITATION: Hook, No. 10, heavy and with a long shank; body, dubbing of white fur, picked out so as to give the artificial a frowsy appearance; wing cases, pale yellowish nails from a Jungle Cock feather; legs or hackle, the palest of honey dun; tails, honey dun hackle, the finest procurable.

The Catalog

RED QUILL NYMPH

Order—*Ephemeroptera* Genus—*Iron*
Family—*Heptageniidae* Species—*pleuralis*

DESCRIPTION: Thorax, greyish brown; tergites, greyish brown with darker brown joinings; sternites, pale yellowish brown; tails, brownish and banded with darker brown; legs, brown with darker spots, giving a mottled appearance; gills, plate-like and conspicuous, brown above and paler beneath.

REMARKS: This is another flat nymph commonly found under stones in the swift riffles. In appearance it resembles the Ginger Quill Nymph very much, except that it is somewhat darker in color; its gills are also more pronounced and it has two tails.

IMITATION: Hook, No. 12; body, first tied loosely with yellowish brown wool, leaving a tuft about an inch long extending out towards the rear; over this yellowish wool underbody spirally wrap stripped peacock quill, then double back the wool strand on the underside towards the front, which will produce a two toned effect, that is, mottled brown above and paler beneath; the whole is then saturated with lacquer or Duco and when almost dry pressed flat; legs, brown and black moosemane; tails, mandarin or wood duck fibres; wing cases, nail from a Jungle Cock feather.

* * *

BROWN QUILL NYMPH

Order—*Ephemeroptera* Genus—*Siphlonurus*
Family—*Baetidae* Species—*quebecensis*

DESCRIPTION: Thorax, brown and enlarged; tergites, brown; sternites, yellowish; legs, yellowish brown; tails, yellowish brown with a dark traverse band near the center; gills on sides of abdomen, flat and brown.

REMARKS: This nymph ranges freely about in slow moving water and quite often is found among the weeds. Its broad, webbed tail serves as a powerful tail fin, and it swims actively about, darting here and there with the swiftness of a young pickerel. Somewhat similar species are found among the genus *Isonychia;* however, these are found under stones and are dark reddish brown in color.

IMITATION: Hook, No. 14; body, dubbing of yellowish brown fur, enlarged at the thorax; legs, brown moosemane; wing pads, nail from a Jungle Cock feather; tails, yellowish brown hackle clipped to shape.

PLATE XXIV.

Brown Quill Nymph   Golden Spinner Nymph

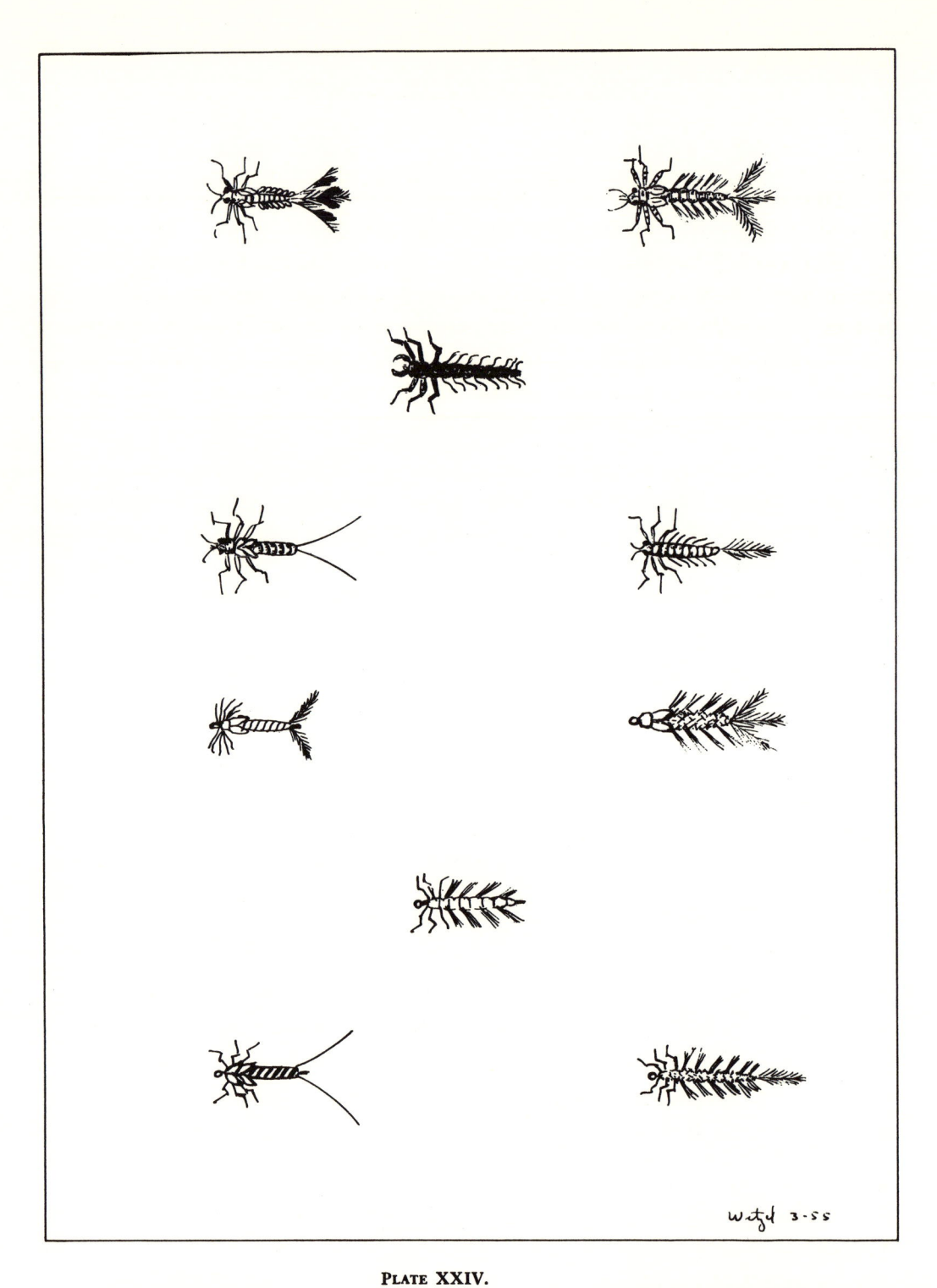

Fish Fly Nymph

Yellow Sally Nymph   Alder Fly Nymph

The Catalog

GOLDEN SPINNER NYMPH

Order—*Ephemeroptera*   Genus—*Potamanthus*
Family—*Ephemeriidae*   Species—*distinctus*

DESCRIPTION: Thorax and abdomen, deep purplish red; legs, reddish brown; tails, reddish brown; gills on sides, hair-like.

REMARKS: This nymph burrows in the sand, trash, and gravel on the stream bed. It favors large, fast flowing waters, and emerges around the end of June, at which time the artificial will prove the most successful.

IMITATION: Hook, No. 12 long shank; body, purplish red wool dubbing; hackle, Palmer style, with dark brown hackle clipped short; legs, dark brown moosemane; tails, fine dark brown hackle tips.

* * * *

FISH FLY NYMPH

Order—*Megaloptera*   Genus—*Chauliodes*
Family—*Corydalidae*   Species—*serricornis*

DESCRIPTION: Head, thorax, and abdomen, black; legs, black; gills or lateral filaments on sides, black but without the hair-like tufts at the base as in the hellgrammite.

REMARKS: The fish fly larva is found hanging to the submerged brush and logs in the slower moving streams. I have taken some nice trout on the artificial, but it appears to be most successful when tied in the smaller sizes.

IMITATION: Hook, No. 12, long shank; body, skunk fur dubbing; hackle, Palmer style, with a black hackle clipped short; legs, black moosemane.

* * * *

YELLOW SALLY NYMPH

Order—*Plecoptero*   Genus—*Isoperla*
Family—*Perlidae*   Species—*bilineata*

DESCRIPTION: General color, yellow; sternites, yellow; tergites, yellow with brown joinings; tails, yellow; antennae, yellow.

REMARKS: This nymph is found under stones in cold, swift mountain streams. It resembles the nymph of the Light Stone fly *Isoperla signata,* and the imitation given below will prove acceptable for both species.

IMITATION: Hook, No. 14 long shank; body, antenna, legs and tail, yellow moosemane; wing pads, nail from a Jungle Cock feather.

ALDER FLY NYMPH

Order—*Megaloptera*   Genus—*Sialis*
Family—*Sialidae*   Species—*infumata*

DESCRIPTION: Head and thorax, yellow; abdomen, brown; gills on sides, hairy and whitish; legs, yellow; tails, whitish yellow.

REMARKS: The Alder Fly larva burrows in the gravel on the stream-bed and seems to prefer large and slow moving waters. Although the larva is not supposed to range about on the stream-bed, the fact remains that they do, for I have taken many trout that had the larva in their stomachs.

IMITATION: Hook, No. 14 long shank; body, brown fur dubbing, with yellow in front near the eye of hook; hackle, Palmer style with a fine white hackle; legs, yellow moosemane; tails, fine white hackle tips.

CHAPTER VII

Emergence Tables

ONE OF THE most practical aids to a fly fisherman is a well constructed emergence table. This table, by the way, is not one of those ephemeral affairs which guarantee the hour and the day when fish bite best; neither is it designed as a cure-all for all your fishing problems; but, if used intelligently and wisely, its value cannot help but be apparent. So many anglers have written me enthusiastic letters concerning its worth, adaptability, and ease of conversion to streams in their own locality, that I felt it should have a definite place here.

Briefly, the value of the table can be described in a few simple words. Its object is to supply you with predetermined information as to just what trout stream insects may be expected over the water on the days you will be fishing. The table will also serve as a layman's means of identifying the hatch.

Anyone can construct such a table for his favorite streams; and, if it has been properly prepared, it will prove invaluable. We plan our trout fishing trips by it, knowing beforehand what fly we can expect to find over the water when we arrive there; and, if we have tied our imitations correctly and the trout took the fly well the year before, then we can reasonably hope to have good sport, providing weather and stream conditions are right.

This emergence table has proved very practical. I have checked the arrival of flies over the same water year after year, and the date of emergence varies but slightly. As an extreme example, one certain Mayfly appeared over the same water, and always on the same date for six successive years. This was the Yellow Drake, *Ephemera varia,* which could always be noticed flying over the waters of Middle Creek in Pennsylvania, on the evening of July the first. The above is the exception rather than the rule, for one can hardly hope to hit it so closely; however, the variation in the majority of cases will prove very slight. I could cite many instances to show that the above is a well established fact, but will content myself with just one more.

On Spring Creek in Pennsylvania the Green, Grey, and Black Drakes, *Ephemera guttulata,* are usually over the water between May 28th and May 30th. This insect corresponds to what the English call their May fly, while here in the East it is known under a variety of names. In Pennsylvania, it is locally termed the Shad Fly on such streams as Penns Creek, Middle Creek, Fishing Creek, Spring Creek, Brodheads Creek and others, while on the Beaverkill, Schoharie, and Ausable in New York State, the insect is known as the Coffin Fly. However, regardless of such colloquialisms, the insect should be known under its rightful name of being either a Green, Grey, or Black Drake, not Shad Flies or Coffin Flies, which offer no clue to the angler as to what stage the insect is in; after all, why should it be changed when these same Green, Grey, and Black Drakes were so designated by that well known angler, A. Nelson Cheney, in the columns of "Shooting and Fishing" over fifty years ago. To quote Cheney: "The May fly or Green Drake is familiar to all anglers. The Grey Drake is the metamorphosis of the female Green Drake, and the purple or blackish drake is the metamorphosis of the male Green Drake." But let us get back to emergence dates.

In 1934, when I first described *Ephemera guttulata,* in the *Pennsylvania Angler,* I mentioned that this insect appeared in prodigious numbers on Spring Creek around the 30th of May. Hass Lose of Bellefonte, Pennsylvania, has been yearly checking its arrival on this stream, and has found that the yearly variation in arrival is slight, although May 28th would more nearly approximate the average date. Anglers now come from all parts of the country to fish the Paradise, their arrival timed beforehand to coincide with the appearance of the insect.

In constructing such an emergence table, the one furnished at the end of this chapter will prove of value in being used as a master; that is, it can be revised for any deviations in emergence dates noted in your locality.

It should be brought out that insects occur on all the trout streams of North America, but not all of them on every stream. Some streams have predominately Mayflies; others, stone flies or caddis flies; while still others have a combination of all. Those listed in the emergence table of this chapter are from common, large hatches having a wide distribution. It will be apparent by this time that the fly fisher is not interested in any rare or new species; what he strives for is representative artificial flies, copied after the most common and widely distributed species. It should also be brought out that the insects listed in the so-called master emergence table are not the only ones that are of value to the fly fisher—far from it. There are literally hundreds of species having a wide distribution that have not yet been seriously considered

Emergence Tables

and classified; and again, there are innumerable cases in which fairly common species have a much wider distribution than is generally known. The fly fisher will have to use his judgment in selecting those trout stream insects which he feels worthy to occupy a place in the emergence table. If his fishing is confined more or less to one certain stream, then he would do well to include all large hatches on which he has definite knowledge that trout feed. Certain genera, of course, have species which are almost identical, both as to size and color; and in such cases the imitation fly should have incorporated in its make-up the chief characteristics of both insects. The date that both flies are over the water, however, should be recorded in the emergence table.

I should like to emphasize the importance of recording in the emergence table those observations made while on the stream. For instance, in the remarks column one should include all those little details, even if they appear to be of minor importance at the time. Later on you may be thankful that they were included, for often they prove of paramount importance. Use either a loose leaf book or a card index for filing. A suggested form is the following.

EMERGENCE TABLE

DATE_____ P.M._____ A.M._____
Body of water_____
Locality_____
Type of insect_____
Common name_____
Scientific name_____
Size of hatch.................Large_____Medium_____Small_____
Length to tip of wings_____

Description of insect:
- Body_____
- Wings_____
- Tail_____
- Legs_____
- Egg sack_____

Description of imitation:
- Hook No._____
- Body_____
- Wings_____
- Tail_____
- Hackle_____
- Egg sack_____

Were trout taking the insect ....Yes_____No_____
Confirmed by post mortem ....Yes_____No_____
Character of stream-bed_____
Speed of water ....Fast_____Medium_____Slow_____
Temperature of water_____
Temperature of air_____
Type of day ....Bright_____Cloudy_____
Remarks: _____
_____

I have found that the best method—immediately after catching a trout stream insect—is to decide on the spot what the most satisfactory materials are for imitating it; in fact, I generally tie up the artificial on the streamside, before any of the colors of the insect change or fade. What does it matter if the trout are jumping furiously? They will do it again. Anglers these days are not fishing for fish, but for sport. If we added up the cost per pound of all the trout taken, it would run into a staggering amount. So what does it matter after all, if we take time off during the height of the hatch, to sit down and tie up a fly which may give us much pleasure later on.

The following emergence table originally appeared in the columns of the *Pennsylvania Angler*,[1] as well as in my other work, *Practical Fly Fishing*,[2] and my thanks are extended to the publishers in allowing me to reproduce it here. This is the table mentioned earlier in this chapter, which will serve as a "master" in preparing an emergence table for the insects found in your locality.

[1] Published by The Pennsylvania State Fish Commission, Harrisburg, Pa.
[2] Published by The Christopher Publishing House, Boston, Mass.

THE EMERGENCE TABLE

The number in parentheses following the common name of the insect indicates: 1, Mayfly; 2, Caddis Fly; 3, Stonefly; 4, Crane Fly; 5, Miscellaneous.

Common Name	Scientific Name	Habitat	Approx. emergence date in climate corresponding to Pennsylvania's
Little Black Stonefly (3)	*Taeniopteryx fasciata*	Pa., W.Va., Tenn., Mass., N.Y., Minn., Mo., Md., Kan.	Apr. 15
Red Quill (1)	*Iron pleuralis*	N.Y., Pa., N.J., Ont., Quebec	Apr. 16
Little Black Caddis (2)	*Chimarrha atterima*	Pa., Canada, N.Y., N.J., Del., Ind., Ga., Fla., Washington	Apr. 17
Red Legged March Fly (5)	*Bibio femoratus*	Pa., N.Y., N.J.	May 1
Alder Fly (5)	*Sialis infumata*	Quebec, N.S., N.Y., New Eng., N.J., Pa., Wash., Mich., Ill., Minn., Calif.	May 1
Black Midge (5)	*Chironomus lobiferus*	Pa., N.Y., N.J., Ont.	May to Sept.
Light Stone Fly (3)	*Isoperla signata*	Pa., N. Y., N. S.	May 1
Black Quill (1)	*Blasturus cupidus*	Pa., Ohio, N.S., N.F., Ill., Canada, N.Y., N.H., N.C., R.I., N.J., Ont., Quebec, Mass.	May 15
Early Brown Spinner (1)	*Blasturus cupidus*	Same as above	May 16
Yellow Spider (4)	*Antocha saxicola*	Well distributed throughout the northern hemisphere	May 15
Stone Fly (3)	*Perla capitata*	Pa., N.Y., Md., Mass., Minn., Quebec, N.S., Ind., Ill., Mich., Kan., Tenn., N.C.	May 15
Spotted Sedge (2)	*Hydropsyche slossonae*	Pa., N.Y., N.H., Ill.	May 16

Emergence Tables

Common Name	Scientific Name	Habitat	Approx. emergence date in climate corresponding to Pennsylvania's
Pale Evening Dun (1)	*Ephemerella dorothea*	Canada	May 20
March Brown (1)	*Stenonema vicarium*	Pa., N.Y., Quebec, N.B., N.H., Tenn.	May 20
Great Red Spinner (1)	*Stenonema vicarium*	Same as above	May 21
Green Caddis (2)	*Rhyacophila lobifera*	Pa., N.Y., Ill.	May 21
Dark Green Drake (1)	*Hexagenia recurvata*	Pa., N.Y., Mass., Me., W.Va., Mich.	May 21
Brown Drake (1)	*Hexagenia recurvata*	Same as above	May 23
Ginger Quill Dun (1)	*Stenonema fuscum*	Pa., N.Y., Ont., Que., New Brunswick	May 24
Pale Evening Spinner (1)	*Ephemerella dorothea*	Pa., N.Y., N.H., Tenn., Quebec, New Brunswick	May 25
Olive Dun Nymph (1)	*Ephemerella fuscata*	Pa., N.Y., Ind., Que., New Brunswick	May 25
Ginger Quill Spinner (1)	*Stenonema fuscum*	Pa., N.Y., Ont., Que., New Brunswick	May 26
Fish Fly (5)	*Chauliodes serricornis*	Pa., N.Y., Md., Ga., Ohio, Minn.	May 26
Green Drake (1)	*Ephemera guttulata*	Pa., N.Y., Tenn., Ont., Quebec	May 26
Black Drake (1)	*Ephemera guttulata*	Same as above	May 28
Grey Drake (1)	*Ephemera guttulata*	Same as Green Drake	May 28
Iron Blue Dun (1)	*Leptophlebia johnsoni*	Pa., N.Y., N.H., Quebec, Ontario	May 28
Grannon (5)	*Brachycentrus fuliginosus*	Pa., N.Y., Wash., Ont.	May 28
Jenny Spinner (1)	*Leptophlebia johnsoni*	Pa., N.Y., N.H., Quebec, Ontario	May 29
Brown Quill (1)	*Siphlonurus quebecensis*	Pa., N.Y., N.C., Ont., Quebec	June 1
Blue Bottle (5)	*Lucilia caeser*	Commonly distributed	Variable
Whirling Crane Fly (4)	*Tipula bella*	Pa., N.Y., N.J.	June 1
Orange Crane Fly (4)	*Tipula bicornis*	Pa., N.Y., N.J.	June 1
Golden Eyed Gauze Wing (5)	*Chrysopa occulata*	Commonly distributed	Variable
White Mayfly (1)	*Stenonema rubromaculatum*	Pa., N.Y., Mass., Ill., Ont., Quebec, N.B., N.S.	June 2
White Gloved Howdy (1)	*Isonychia albomanicata*	Pa., N.Y., Ont., N.C.	June 27
Yellow Sally (3)	*Isoperla bilineata*	Ohio, Newfoundland to Saskatchewan and N.J. to Col. The common eastern species	June 28
Golden Spinner (1)	*Potomanthus distinctus*	Pa., N.Y., W.Va., Ohio	June 28
Willow or Needle Fly (3)	*Leuctra grandis*	Pa., N.Y., N.J., North Carolina	June 28
Stonefly Nymph (3)	*Acroneuria lycorias*	Pa., N.H., N.Y., Mass., Me., W.Va., Mich., Wisc., Quebec	June 29
Brown Silverhorns (2)	*Athripsodes wetzeli*	Pa., N.Y. Similar species in Wisc. and Ont.	June 30
Big Orange Sedge (2)	*Neuronia postica*	Pa., Ga., Mass., Wisc., New Foundland, Washington, D. C.	July 1
Yellow Drake (1)	*Ephemera varia*	Pa., N.Y., Mich. N.H., Ontario	July 1
White Caddis (2)	*Leptocella exquisita*	Florida to Canada	July 1
Deer Fly (5)	*Chrysops vittatus*	Eastern and Northern States	Variable
Green Midge (5)	*Chironomus modestus*	Pa., N.Y., N.J., Ontario	July 4
Scud (5)	*Gammarus minus*	Pa., N.Y.	Variable
Little Damsel Fly Nymph (5)	*Ischnura verticalis*	Pa., N.Y., N.J.	Variable

CHAPTER VIII

Imitating the Natural Insect

THIS chapter will be confined entirely to the methods employed in imitating those insects found along the trout streams.

For a great many years I have made it a point to always carry with me on fishing trips an assortment of fly tying materials, and I would strongly urge the reader to follow this plan. By so doing, one is in a position to copy before their colors fade any of the insects which hover over the water. On more than one occasion when trout refused my every offering, I have sat down by the streamside, brought out the kit and fashioned a fly which immediately began to take fish. The box housing this material need not be any larger than a dry fly box, a size which can easily be tucked into the pocket, and it is amazing the amount of fly tying material that can be stored in such a small space. In selecting the material, one must be governed by anticipated needs.

My kit contains a box of assorted hooks, a spool of tying silk, wax, a vise (sometimes not used), scissors, hackle pliers, dubbing needle, lacquer cement, tinsel (fine gold and silver wire), and the following wing and body material individually packed in small cellophane envelopes: quill feathers (both rights and lefts) in various colors, small fan-wing feathers in various shades and sizes, various speckled and barred feathers, such as mandarin, teal, mallard, etc.; hackles of various shades and sizes; assortments of floss silk, angora yarn, wool, fur, chenille, raffia grass, plastacele cut into thin strips; moosemane, jungle cock feathers, peacock herl, and various shades of peacock quill previously stripped from the eye feather.

No one can tie an attractive fly without proper materials, and in this connection the following hints may prove helpful.

Hackles are a proverbial source of trouble. Of late years it is almost impossible to get a good dry fly neck, and if one is procurable, buy it regardless of the cost. Some fly tying concerns have no hesitation at all in palming off on the unsuspecting amateur supposedly good dry fly necks which are absolutely worthless for this class of work. Insist on having a number of necks

94   *Trout Flies—Naturals and Imitations*

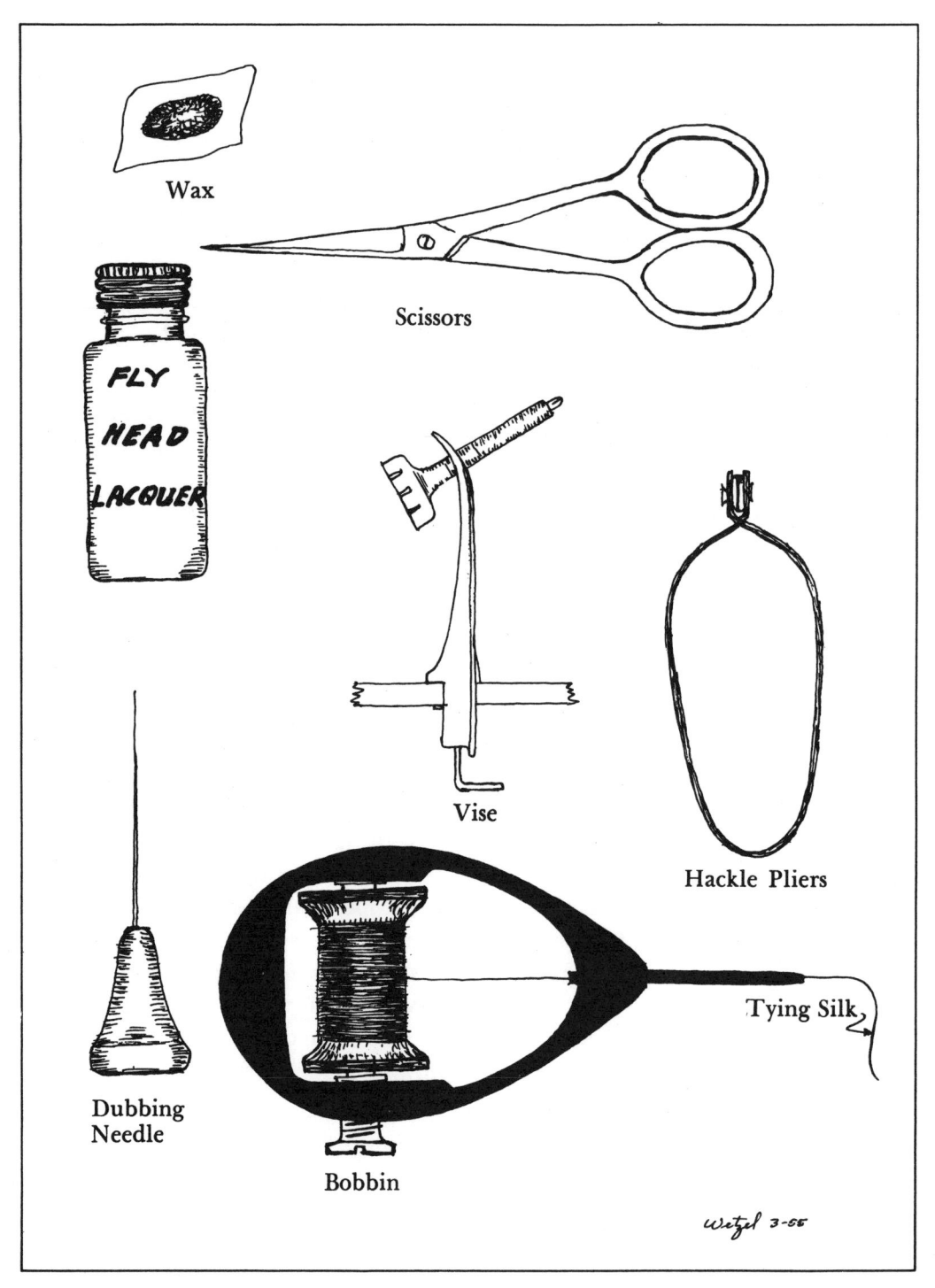

PLATE XXV. Fly Tyers' Tools

Imitating the Natural Insect

sent you for examination—pay a deposit if required—and then select those which are suitable. Concerns which will not countenance such a request do not deserve business from the fly tyer, and further trade with them should be stopped immediately.

Hackles which have a lot of curly down at the root of the stem are invariably soft. The ideal dry fly hackle has a minimum of short, straight down at the root of the stem, more in the nature of fibres; it is long, thin stemmed, stiff and shining; and when held to the light and bent so that the fibres separate, there will be noticed an absence of flue or webbing extending upwards from the base of each fibre. This flue or webbing is most undesirable from the point of view of the dry fly tyer, for it soaks up water like a sponge. All hackles have it to a greater or lesser degree; however, a minimum amount will prove the most satisfactory for dry flies. For wet flies, the softer the hackle, the better.

One common fault among amateur fly tyers is to use a tying silk that is too heavy. A fine grade is absolutely essential to properly fashion the delicate duns and spinners found over the water. For ordinary trout flies, use nothing heavier than size 4-0, and for very small flies 6-0 will give satisfactory results. It is now possible to procure tying silk already waxed, a boon to those fly tyers who experience difficulty in preventing the thread from breaking while waxing it.

Hooks for dry flies should be of the finest and lightest wire obtainable. The turned-up, tapered eye is to be preferred since it is easier to fasten off when applying the whip finish. For wet flies, the turned down eye, flat bend, will prove very satisfactory.

Feathers from water birds are without doubt superior to all others for dry fly wings, mainly due to the great amount of natural oil which makes them more impervious to water.

Teal, mallard, and mandarin side feathers are ideal for tail material, for the mottled effect of such fibres closely approximates the segments in the tails of the natural insect.

In imitating insects whose bodies present a black and yellowish ringed appearance, nothing proves superior to peacock quill. This quill is obtained by scraping away the flue from those strands or herl or fibres located at the eye of a peacock tail feather or by quickly dipping in chlorox. A blend of various colored strands of moosemane will also achieve the same effect; however, it is most suitable for the smaller flies.

To obtain a transparent body, I have found nothing yet to equal Plastacele, a DuPont product that resembles heavy cellophane. This material takes dye very readily and a variety of colors are easily obtained. The material is then cut into thin strips, approximately one-sixteenth of an inch wide, which is used to form the body of the fly.

To obtain a mottled body effect in keeping with certain insects, a dubbing composed of various colored furs will prove satisfactory. Use only the soft fur next to the skin, as the outer hair is too coarse. This fur should be cut up into very fine pieces, blended to give the correct shade, then twisted on the waxed tying silk and the body formed. Spun fur, angora yarn, or white rabbit fur dyed in various shades makes a body irresistible to trout.

Certain floss silks, etc., when saturated with water, undergo a color change, and it should be borne in mind that only this saturated shade should be used when imitating the insect.

Quite often the wings of certain insects present a mottled appearance, which can best be imitated by the speckled side feathers of the mallard, teal, and mandarin duck.

Imitations of the stone fly group should be dressed with long wings to lie flat over the top of the body.

The wings of Mayflies are imitated in a variety of ways: (1) Upright or forward wings, to represent the insect as it rests or floats on the water. Wings so constructed are normally fashioned from right and left quill feathers. My personal preference is for the forward wing, as it seems to float and cock better on the water. (2) Rolled wings, which are constructed from a speckled side feather (such as a mallard, teal, or mandarin duck) to imitate those smaller Mayflies having mottled wings. (3) Fan wings, especially used for imitating the larger Mayflies having mottled wings. Like the others, they represent the insect as it rests or floats on the water. Fan wings are constructed from matched curled feathers which flare away from each other. Their main advantage lies in their use for large flies, in that they are more stable and will not keel over so quickly on the surface of the water, as does the upright wing. (4) Spent wings, usually constructed from hackle points extending out at right angles to the body, so designed to imitate the Mayfly as it falls exhausted and inert on the water, its life cycle completed. Any Mayfly in the spinner or imago stage can be imitated spent, or resting, depending on the preference of the fly tyer.

The wings imitating the caddis fly group should extend beyond the bend of the hook, and should slope roof-like over the body. To greater or lesser degree this applies to the fish fly and the alder as well.

Imitations of the crane fly group are normally tied with hackle point wings extending out at right angles to the body. This is in keeping with the wings of the insect while at rest. The long legs can be imitated by extra long saddle hackles.

In fly tying there are a number of undesirable operations that should be

Imitating the Natural Insect 97

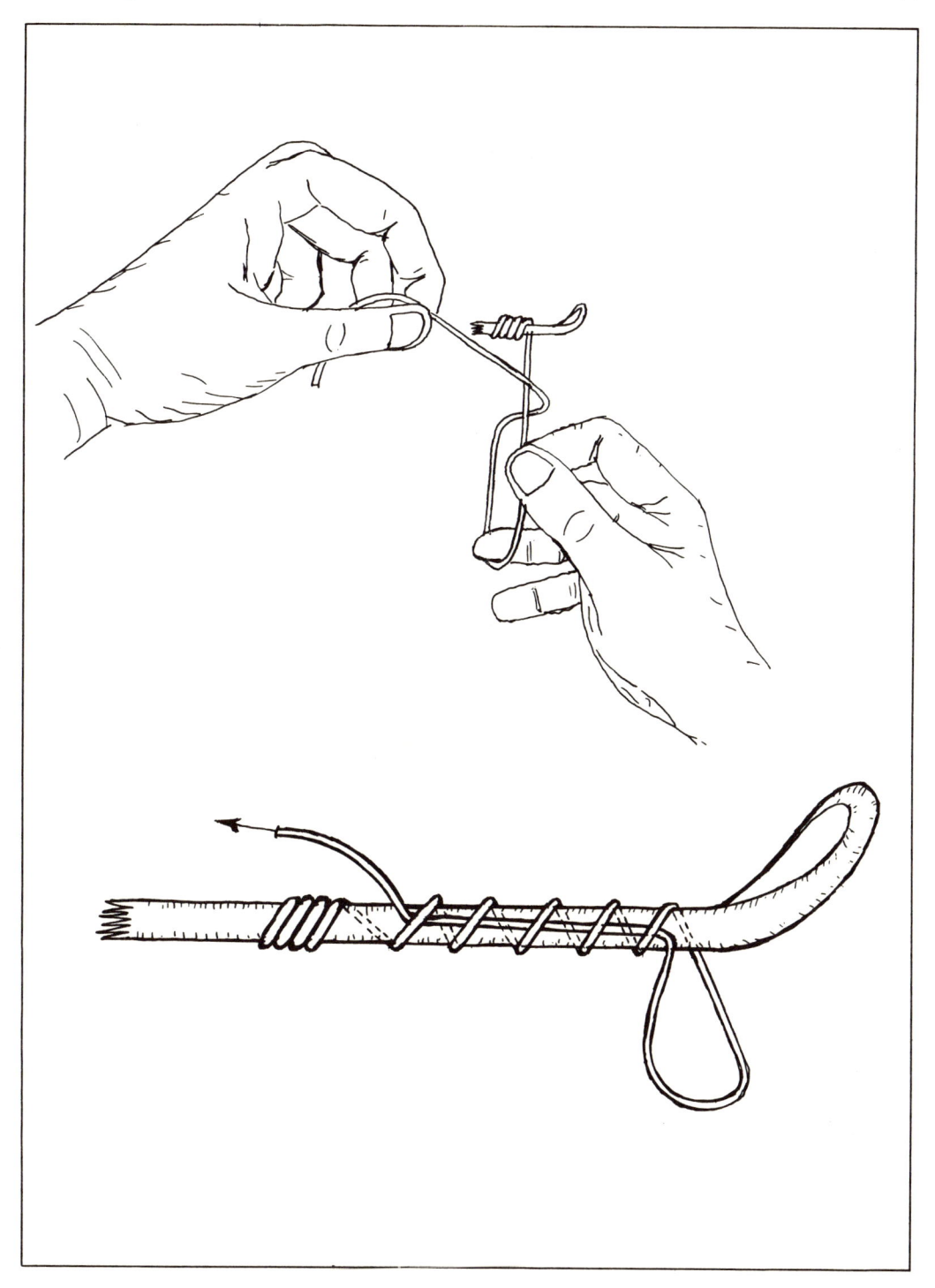

PLATE XXVI. The Whip Finish.

avoided if neatness and a realistic effect is to be obtained. Don't finish off a fly with half hitches, which are neither neat nor secure. Refer to the sketch and learn to tie the whip finish—the professional fly tyers knot.

Bulges at the end of the body are caused by tying in a too thick material. If chenille is used, the flue should be removed and the exposed thread core fastened in with the tying silk. Materials such as raffia grass, quill, Plastacele, etc., should have their ends cut on a bevel and fastened at the narrow part; the same applies to tinsels. Wool, angora yarn, and dubbing should be thinned out before fastening in.

When winding on a floss silk body, never twist the material, for a bulge is sure to result.

To prevent wings from splitting, hold the sections tightly together over the hook; bring the tying silk up and down between the fingers and do not release wings until they are fastened on the hook by at least three turns of the tying silk.

To insure that certain body material will entirely cover the shank of the hook, it is well to fasten it in at the eye, winding out to the bend, then back again before fastening off.

When wings are constructed from right and left quill feathers, avoid using the first primary as it is too stiff.

Before fastening in the hackle on a dry fly don't neglect to pull it between the thumb and fore finger, so that the fibres will stand out from the stem in a normal manner. Wet fly hackles should be bearded, not wound on; that is, a group of fibers are stripped from a hackle and this bundle is then tied in on the underside.

In starting a fly, make it a point to leave a space of at least an eighth of an inch back of the eye for winding on the hackle and forming the head. The crowding of wings and hackle too close to the eye is a sure sign of the amateur.

Tying A Dry Fly

The following steps illustrate the order of procedure that I use when tying a dry fly. Refer to the sketch, which should help in gaining a clear idea of the steps involved. The fly will be tied with forward wings.

Place the hook in the vise and tear off about twenty inches of tying silk that has previously been well waxed. Lay the tying silk on the shank of the hook, winding over its own end with a few turns. See Sketch 1. Clip the one pair of hackle pliers near the free end of the tying silk, letting it hang so that the hands will henceforth be free. Throughout the construction of the fly this

Imitating the Natural Insect

pair of pliers will be continuously employed in this one duty, namely that of keeping the tying silk taut.

Select a hackle so that the length of fiber is approximately equal to the length of hook. Strip off the useless down near the root and tie it on the far side of the shank, with the dull or inside of the hackle facing you. This feature is to insure the forward slope of the fibers after the hackle is wound on. Sketch 2 illustrates the construction of the fly at this stage.

From two primary feathers or quills, cut out sections as shown in the illustration. Place the convex faces together, and tie them on the shank of the hook about one-eighth of an inch back of the eye, as shown on Sketch 3. Bind down the butt ends of the wings and cut away the useless fibers. Pass the tying silk in front of the wings and work them into a more upright position, so that they do not lie too low over the eye of the hook. Carefully divide the wings with the dubbing needle, being careful not to split the fibers, and with the thumb, press them open until they lie quite flat. Pass the tying silk between the wings and with a figure of eight tying, secure in the desired position. Sketch 4 shows a top view of the fly at this stage.

Wind the tying silk towards the bend of the hook, where the body material, tail whisks, and ribbing wire should be secured in place with a few turns. Now move the tying silk forward near the eye of the hook, letting it hang as before. See Sketch 5.

Grasp the body material in the right hand and wind it on tightly and smoothly, working towards the eye of the fly and forming a slight taper. Now with the tying silk bind down the body material and with the scissors cut off the execess end. See Sketch 6.

Spirally wind on the ribbing wire, reversing the direction from which the body material was wound on, and taking care that it is wound on uniform spaces. Fasten the end of the ribbing wire with a few turns of the tying silk and cut off the excess end. Sketch 7 represents the stage of the fly at this point.

Now clip the other pair of hackle pliers to the tip of the hackle and wind it on, first with a few turns back of the wings, and then bringing it forward and completing the winding in the front. Work the tying silk forward through the fibers, fasten the hackle tip with a few turns, and cut off the excess waste. See Sketch 8.

For those who have difficulty in fastening off because of the hackle fibers getting in the way, the following method is recommended. Procure a piece of cardboard about an inch-and-a-half square, and with the dubbing needle punch out a hole at the center. Run the free end of the tying silk through this hole; grasp the end and keep it taut; remove the hackle pliers and slip this cardboard up and over the eye of the hook. See Sketch 9.

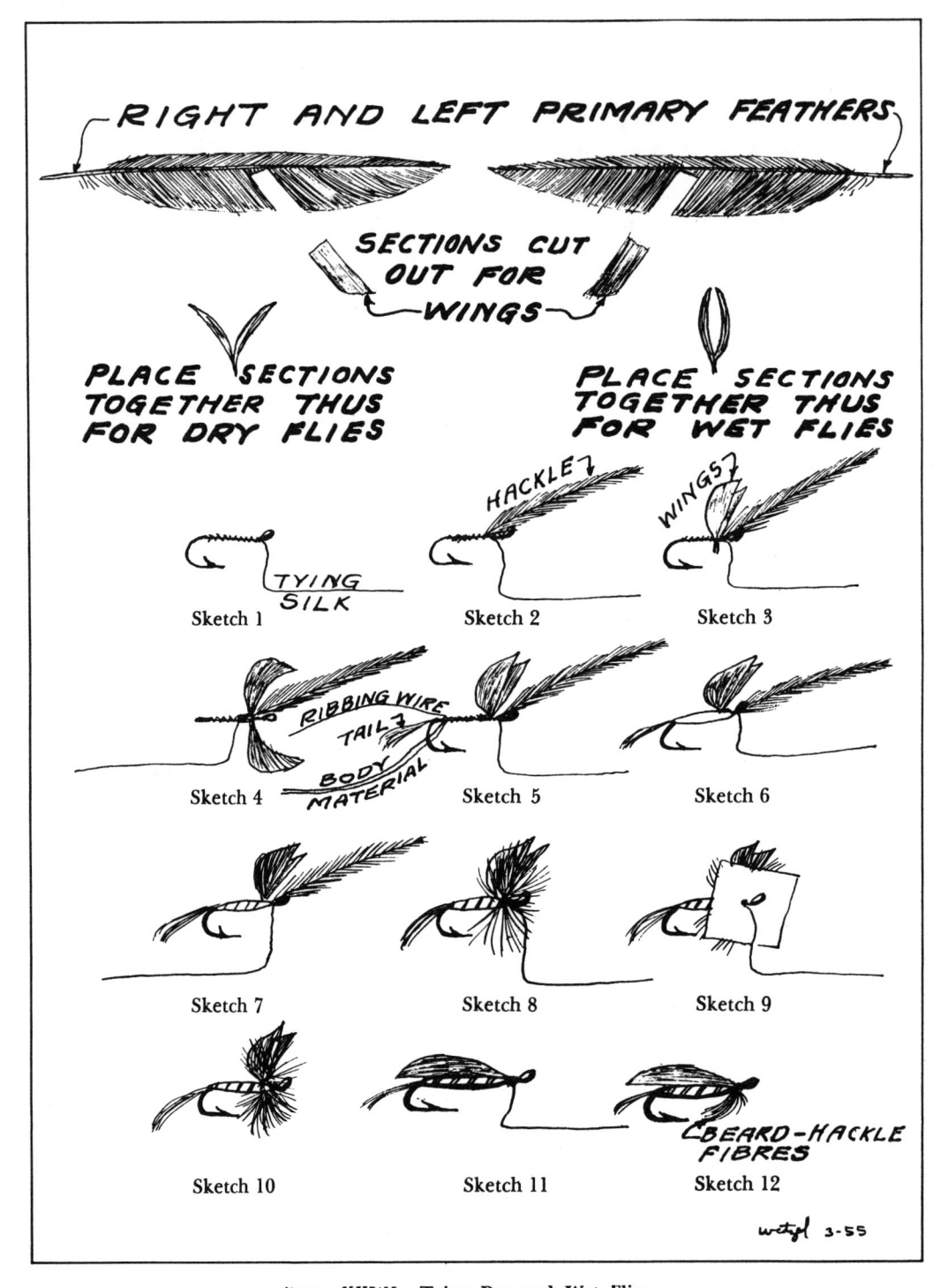

PLATE XXVII. Tying Dry and Wet Flies.

Imitating the Natural Insect

The hackle fibers on the other side of the cardboard are now out of the way, and the head should be formed, after which the whip finish or fastening off knot should be applied. Finally clip off the excess end of the tying silk, put a drop of lacquer on the head; remove the cardboard and the dry fly is finished. See Sketch 10.

TYING A WET FLY

Wet flies are tied in a manner very similar to dry flies. First, the body ribbing and tail is constructed; then the wings, concave faces together, are tied in as shown in Sketch 11. Fibers are next stripped from a hackle, and this small bundle is then tied in on the underside, i.e., bearded. Bearding a fly is far preferable to winding on a hackle; one does not need to be too much concerned about the size of fibers used; and being tied in on the underside only, the fly will sink more readily. Finish off in the usual way. Sketch 12 shows the finished wet fly.

TYING A NYMPH

I developed the methods and materials used for tying Mayfly and stone fly nymphs a number of years ago; and when they are constructed as described below, they will prove excellent fish takers.

Peacock quill is a fine body material for certain nymphs; however due to its short length, I have discarded it almost entirely in favor of moosemane.

The method of tying a stone fly nymph will now be briefly described. Refer to the various figures, which will help to visualize the manner of putting the nymph together.

Fasten in the floss silk, body material, moosemane tail, and feelers, as shown in Figure A.

With floss silk build up the body to the shape of the natural nymph. See Figure B.

Near the bend of the hook, fasten in the brown and yellow moosmane. Figure C.

Wind on the brown moosemane first; fasten it at the eye of the fly; then spirally wind on the yellow, which will give the ringed or banded appearance of the prototype. See Figure D.

From two jungle cock feathers (Figure E) detach the nails, which serve as wing cases, and tie them in as shown in plan view, Figure F, one in front of the other. If the nails do not split in the center, separate them with a knife.

Detach a number of strands of moosemane, which will imitate the legs, and place them underneath the fly, as shown in Figure G. Take a couple of loose turns with the tying silk around the hook and the moosemane, and then

102   *Trout Flies—Naturals and Imitations*

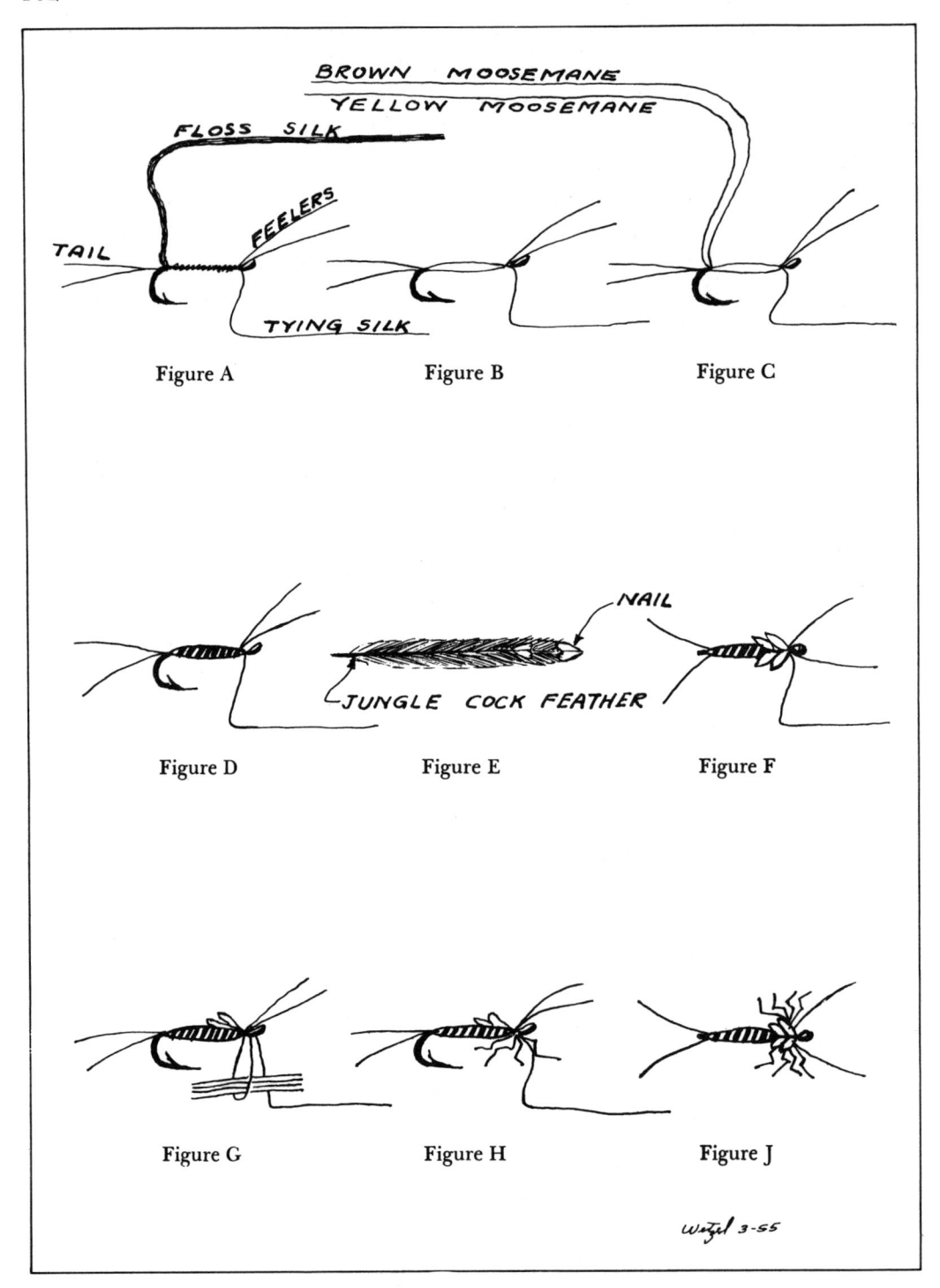

PLATE XXVIII. Tying a Nymph.

Imitating the Natural Insect

guiding the moosemane between the thumb and first finger of the left hand, which also encloses the hook shank, pull vertically downwards. The pressure of the thread cutting into the moosemane will cause the fibers to spread out, after which the legs should be secured in position with a few turns of the tying silk. Fasten off with the whip finish; cut out the excess legs; place a drop of lacquer on the head, and the nymph is complete.

Figure H shows an elevation of the completed nymph, and Figure J shows it in plan view.

CHAPTER IX

Transplanting Stream Insects

MAY FLIES can be transplanted from one stream to another, providing the same stream-bed surroundings are obtained; it might also be well to remark that insects indigenous to limestone streams will not thrive in those of free stone, and vice versa.

On Middle Creek in Pennsylvania, some twenty years ago, I introduced the Green, Gray, and Black Drakes from Penns Creek, a distance of about twenty miles away These flies quickly adjusted themselves to their new environment and multiplied very rapidly, hatches now being almost as large as on the parent stream.

Before proceeding with the manner in which these flies were transplanted, it might be well to briefly review the life stages of this insect, in order that the reader may have a clear conception of the difficulties encountered.

The nymph of this fly, *Ephemera guttulata*, burrows in the mud and gravel of the streambed. It is whitish yellow in appearance, has three hairy tails, and when fully grown measures about an inch in length. About the end of May the nymph rises to the surface of the water, where the nymphal skin splits open, permitting the fly to escape from its shuck. At times the process of extricating itself from this skin proves very difficult; many insects still have bits of it adhering to them a few hours after this metamorphosis. At this time the fly is very weak—the organs of flight are not yet firmly developed—and it immediately makes its way to land, quite often coming down and resting on the surface of the water if the shore line is some distance away; others will not even attempt to fly, but will ride down on the current until they reach the shore line, whereupon they will fly up on the brush and blades of grass at the water's edge. In the majority of cases, the fly will hang upside down for a few hours on the foliage until its wings grow strong, whereupon it takes wing, and rises higher and higher, until it is finally lost in the tree tops. In this sub-imago stage both male and female flies are known as Green Drakes.

The above is sufficient to gain a clear understanding of the matter, but to make the history complete, I might mention that a couple of days later the Green Drake, while still resting on the tree tops, sheds this sub-imago skin, and then reappears over the water, just before dark, in almost unbelievable numbers. In this imago stage, the male fly is now known as the Black Drake, and the female as the Grey Drake.

The first experiment in an attempt to transplant *Ephemera guttulata* resulted in a discouraging failure. I tried to transplant the nymphs, which was the wrong thing to do. The work of collecting them was very great; they were exceedingly difficult to locate; then again, many were injured while shoveling them out of the mud and sand on the stream bed. Only about twenty-five were secured, and it is quite probable that a majority of these died while trying to adjust themselves to their new environment.

Somewhat discouraged over their failure to appear during the next few years, I nevertheless determined to try it again. This time I would transplant the fly in the sub-imago stage.

The following year, about the fifteenth of May, I constructed a large cage made out of window screening material. The box was roughly about four feet long, two feet wide, and two feet deep, having a hinged lid on the top. Three loose false bottoms were also provided, their purpose being explained later. Another cage, ten by ten by ten inches, made out of the same material, was used for the purpose of collecting the insects.

About the latter part of May, I received word that the Green Drakes were beginning to appear over the waters of Penns Creek. I immediately drove over, made a survey of the situation, and congratulated myself that I had arrived at the proper time. The fly was not yet on in abundance; however, a few could be seen riding down on the surface of the water, while here and there others were making a weak, unsteady flight to the shore line. It might be well here to remark that when a Mayfly is flying through the air as if it had some definite objective in view, it can usually be regarded as being in the sub-imago stage.

That afternoon approximately five hundred were taken and transferred to the larger cage, which was provided with damp grass and green alder twigs. These flies were all picked as they hung wings downwards from the underside of the foliage and blades of grass bordering the stream.

Extreme care was used in capturing them, so that none would be injured, and it was felt that the best method of carrying them would be to provide horizontal partitions made out of screening; in other words, the first layer of Mayflies—totaling five hundred—were placed on the bottom of the cage, with plenty of damp grass and space in between to provide adequate ventilation.

Transplanting Stream Insects

About six inches above the bottom of the box, the false bottom or horizontal partition was then sewed into position along the periphery, in preparation for the next group.

Quite a few mayflies were also taken that night. The car was driven close to the water's edge, and a large white sheet was spread on the ground some distance in the front, so that the lights would shine on it; after it grew dark, the Mayflies, attracted by the lights, were picked off the sheet.

Fearing that the insects might not survive the close quarters in which they were confined—for here and there dead ones could be seen—I was extremely anxious to wind up operations by noon the following day.

In the morning the Green Drakes were coming off the water in great numbers, and two hours work enabled me to fill the cage to capacity. I estimated roughly that I had now captured some twenty-five hundred flies, and while transporting them to their future home, I had rather grave misgivings as to the number which would survive the ordeal, for the day was hot and sultry. However, in liberating them, I was overjoyed to discover that the mortality rate was quite low; in fact less than one hundred had succumbed. This was probably due to the extreme care used in picking them, keeping them constantly in the shade, and providing them with plenty of moisture. The proportion of females to males was about three to one.

One evening later, just before dark, the flies—now all transformed into Grey and Black Drakes—started their erratic mating flight over the water, and the prospects of a future crop appeared most hopeful.

Feeling that the experiment could not help but be a success, I wrote to the Pennsylvania Fish Commission, urging them to consider the advisability of stocking the North Branch of Middle Creek with brown trout. I might say that this creek is rather warm; however, it is tributary to Swift Run, a cold water mountain stream unexcelled for brook trout, and I felt confident that if brown trout were placed in it, they would survive and thrive. In my letter I mentioned that Middle Creek contained an abundance of minnow and insect life, with plenty of cover; however no mention was made of my efforts to transplant the Green Drake.

Consideration was given to my letter, and the Board sent around one of their stream survey men to make an investigation. His findings confirmed my predictions that the stream would be acceptable for brown trout, with the result that Middle Creek was accordingly stocked and put on the list for future yearly stocking. How well the fish have adjusted themselves to their new environment can best be judged from the great number of anglers who now yearly fly fish the stream.

For four successive years I was on Middle Creek from the twenty-eighth of May until the thirtieth, the period in which I estimated the fly would emerge from the water, but the results again proved most discouraging. The newly transplanted brown trout had taken hold well, but the only insects that were abroad were the Pale Evening Duns, *Ephemerella dorothea;* the March Browns, *Stenonema vicarium;* and the Ginger Quill Duns, *Stenonema fuscum.* Nowhere were the Green Drakes in evidence.

While driving home that night, I had a sudden inspiration. Perhaps the flies were emerging later than the time at which I anticipated their arrival. All evidence seemed to point that way, for the Pale Evening Duns, the March Browns, and the Ginger Quills all appeared on other streams around the same vicinity approximately a week earlier than on Middle Creek. If those flies were a week late, then it was also reasonable to presume that the Green Drakes might be doing the same.

The following year I timed my arrival to be on Middle Creek from June the second until the sixth.

On June the second, while fly fishing the Creek, I noticed a large insect that had sprung from the water and was leisurely riding down on the current. It was too far away to distinguish it clearly; however, it had proceeded only a distance of some ten feet, when a large brown trout rose slowly to the surface, opened up his mouth, and gulped it down.

From the studied and deliberate way in which the trout took the fly it appeared that he would rise again, since it was apparent that the fish was definitely feeding on insects. I don't recall what fly I had on the leader at the time, but no sooner had it floated over the fish, than he rose and took it solidly. The trout was a large one, quite active, racing here and there, but after a time I got in control of the situation, and very soon thereafter led it into the net. It was a beautiful, well conditioned fish, twenty inches long, and one of the largest I have ever taken from Middle Creek.

Scrambling out on the bank, I knocked the fish on the head, took out the knife, and made a post mortem examination on the spot. From the stomach contents, it was apparent that the fly the trout had just taken was a Green Drake, and to say that I was delighted would be putting it mildly. An examination of the foliage bordering the stream disclosed numerous Green Drakes clinging to the underside, and the following evening we had a great mayfly carnival. As a matter of information, these flies appeared in the greatest numbers about a half a mile downstream from where they were originally liberated. Since that time they have appeared regularly each season, and a great many anglers visiting Middle Creek now time their arrival to coincide with the date of emergence.

* * * * *

Transplanting Stream Insects

When excerpts of the above paper on transplanting Mayflies appeared in the columns of *The Pennsylvania Angler,* I received a letter from my old friend C. K. (Charlie) Fox,* of Harrisburg, who had been working on the redistribution and the following is his report to The Fly Fisher's Club of Harrisburg.

REDISTRIBUTION OF MAYFLIES
By Charles K. Fox

The only situation which is responsible for a fine rise of the better trout of a given stream is the presence in quantity of some large insect floating on the surface of the water. When this condition does not exist, the most cherished fish feed below the water's surface and are not tempted by the dry fly.

Of all the hatches, the Green Drake—*guttulata*—enjoys the reputation of bringing about the ultimate in angling for trout.

Roger Wooley, in his excellent book, *Modern Trout Fly Dressing*, writes; "The sight of practically all the trout in a stream rising well at the same time has given the impression that the trout's "silly season" is the duffer's opportunity to make large captures. This will not be found always or even often the case, and frequently just as much skill will be found to be necessary when fishing the mayfly, as when fishing the imitations of the smaller *Ephemera*. So let not the mayfly carnival be looked upon as a time for great slaughter, but rather as a time for extra careful fishing for the big fish of the stream, the fish that may have an inclination to turn cannibals and that rarely give the opportunity of their capture with smaller flies. Happy is the angler who can be on a trout stream daily from the beginning to the end of a mayfly season, with a good rise of fly on, for most interesting and instructive will be his experiences, if only he is not too keen on catching fish and has the observant eye to notice the wonders that will unfold themselves."

Ironically this spectacular hatch, so highly regarded, frequently pursued and carefully observed by the angler, does not exist in every cold water stream or even every section of Pennsylvania. The fact that it marks its appearance in all of the limestone streams and some of the freestone waters

---

* Charlie Fox is one of the best known fishermen in Pennsylvania. It was he who prepared the original paper advocating miniature plugs for smallmouth bass, a paper so well received that it marked the beginning of the use of light lures in this country. He has since authored the classic on the subject, *Advanced Bait Casting*. I have fished with Charlie and his friends, Bob McCafferty, Alex Sweigart, Clayton Peters, Don Martin, Lew Kunkel, and others, and they are among the keenest anglers in this country. By coincidence he and I are working together on this book, my fourth, for he is now the Executive Editor of The Stackpole Company.

of the central counties of the state and some other isolated sections, but does not appear in the great limestone section of southeastern Pennsylvania prompted the thought that it might be successfully transplanted to this area where it is nonexistent. Members of the Fly Fisher's Club of Harrisburg were determined to make an honest effort to introduce the insect.

There are three possible methods of approach in the matter of redistribution. The first is to transfer the nymph. In view of the fact that the larva of the insect in question is so difficult to capture, this is not practical. In regard to the nymph Dr. Lyte, eminent angler of Allentown, writes as follows in a personal letter: "Some years ago a friend and myself gathered a bucket of mud from the side banks of the Little Lehigh, containing some water and a good number of mayfly nymphs. It was late in the evening, so we put the bucket in the cellar over night. In the meantime the larva emerged and our cellar was full of mayflies. It was our intention to plant them in another stream." He adds that the nymphs were difficult to catch.

The second method is to transplant the fly. In the dun (sub-imago) stage, they are delicate. Spinners (imago) cannot be captured, transplanted and released, for sufficient time does not exist between the nuptual flight and the depositing of the eggs to permit transportation.

The third alternative is to transplant the egg. This method makes it possible to deal in volume and this was the system that the Club elected to adopt.

After missing the hatch on four or five streams in late May and early June of 1946, it appeared that it was over everywhere for the year; then the information was relayed by a long distance telephone call that a heavy hatch of duns was in progress on Honey Creek. A hatch of spinners should follow this emergence by 48 hours.

We chose a spot at an island along the hard road approximately three miles above the point where Honey Creek flows into the Kishacoquillis. There was a wooded area one-quarter of a mile down stream, which should harbor many flies during the molt.

Upon our arrival at six o'clock on the evening of June 9, 1946, it was bright and clear, a condition which brings about a late evening hatch but a concentrated one. Some duns were emerging. Many male spinners were flying about the tree tops but no females were in evidence upon our arrival.

About one hour before dark the female spinners left the foliage almost simultaneously, and the nuptual flight quickly developed. Forty-five minutes before dark the fertilized females descended and started their slow migration up stream, which immediately succeeds the laying of the eggs.

This is a large drake, pale in color and identical in appearance to the

Transplanting Stream Insects

Spring Creek specimen. Along with it was another fine, large drake, dark brown in color and later identified as *Ephemera simulans*.

A boiler one-third full of water was placed on the island. Two men with nets were stationed in each channel beside the island. The flies in their slow cumbersome up-stream migration followed the water course and did not travel over the island. It was our first thought that netting could be accomplished from the island and from a wooden bridge 20 feet above the water, situated 100 yards above the island. It was soon discovered that it was necessary to operate from the water, for the concentrated flight was near the surface and confined its course within the shorelines.

The hatch was heavy. It was possible to swing the net back and forth until a mass of 25 or more flies was in the bag, before emptying into a wash boiler. At times at the peak of activity two or three females were captured with one swipe of the net.

After being dumped into the boilers they quivered on the surface of the water. This action apparently accompanied the expulsion of the egg masses. The eggs fill the thorax up to the head in two parallel sacks. It is our belief that a gas is generated which forces the eggs to drop in masses but not all at one time.

During the 45 minutes of concentrated flight we believe we averaged 15 flies per minutes or 675 per net making a total of 2700 flies. Halford has written that according to microscopic count each female carries slightly over 7000 eggs. On this basis the total number of eggs secured that evening was approximately 19,000,000, 90 per cent *guttulata* eggs and 10 per cent *simulans*.

The following evening was probably more effective, for there were five nets in operation and a refinement was the addition of a removable cloth bottom in each boiler to which great masses of eggs adhered.

Upon arriving at the Letort, approximately two hours later, the following steps were taken. The dead and few dying females were placed in a wire box and submerged, on the theory that some eggs had adhered to the bodies and wings. The milky colored water of the boilers was poured into the stream. The cloth bottoms on which there was a layer of eggs one-eighth of an inch deep were ripped into strips and pegged to the stream bottom. These strips were literally heavy with egg masses. The boilers themselves, to which eggs had adhered, were submerged. Finally the cloth liners of the nets, to which eggs had adhered and which had been transported submerged in buckets, were planted.

Halford has written that the eggs of the Mayfly hatched in nine days in an aquarium.

Dr. B. W. Kunkel, former head of the Biology Department of Lafayette

College, is of the belief that a loss of eggs was suffered due to overcrowding. This could readily be overcome by the insertion of additional cloth bottoms during the netting operation.

The three leading authorities of the United States were requested to comment and pass judgment on this enterprise following the 1946 endeavor. In addition to the method of capture, transportation, and stocking the following facts were set forth. The streams stocked are less than 100 miles distant from the area of great hatches, and about 40 miles further south. The difference in elevation is less than 1000 feet. A mountain range segregates the two. The stream characteristics appear to be similar in respect to bottom and vegetation.

Contents of a letter from Paul R. Needham, Director of Fisheries, Oregon in 1946, formerly of Cornell University and author of *Better Trout Streams:*

> "It seems to me that if conditions were suitable in the area described, *guttulata* should certainly be present, in spite of the fact that the two sections are separated by a mountainous area. Winged forms such as mayflies distribute themselves long distances and if conditions are suitable will usually be found in waters to which they are adapted.
>
> "A number of years ago, we introduced the burrowing mayfly nymph into Mr. E. R. Hewitt's waters on the Neversink River in the Catskills. I do not believe that they ever "took" there because conditions were not suitable. You might write to Mr. E. R. Hewitt about this and ask him if he could give you the latest word on it. His address is 127 E. Twenty-first Street, New York.
>
> "The green drake in nymph form is a burrower in silt beds in both lakes and streams. If the stream that you described did not possess deep beds of silt it is likely that they failed to find conditions suitable, and as a result never developed.
>
> "It seems to me your method of introduction was satisfactory and if conditions had been suitable, they should have developed.
>
> "I, personally, am quite pessimistic about your chances of being able to establish them in an area in which they are not already present. Often times small changes from their home habitat are enough to block success. Your approach was all right and you are correct in the assumption that usually the green drakes require three years in the nymph stage.
>
> "I am sorry that I cannot give you more specific aid in this problem."

Contents of a letter from Charles Wetzel, author of *Practical Fly Fishing:*

> "Your method of redistributing mayflies opened up an entirely new avenue of approach. I had never thought of that angle; however, I don't see why it should not work, providing the eggs were properly fertilized before being put out into the stream. As you know copulation occurs in the air only a short time before the female spinner starts depositing her eggs on the water. I have never been definitely able to determine how the latter operation is accomplished,

Transplanting Stream Insects

although I have caught many female spinners that had two sacks of eggs protruding from her abdomen, which leads me to believe that they are deposited in a mass. What is your theory on this angle? As I mentioned, if the act of copulation occurred before the flies were put into the wash boilers, then your chances of success are very good, providing the same stream bed conditions as applied to the parent stream are encountered. I have found that this is a very important matter. Some streams will just not harbor certain species.

"The fly on Spring Creek is *E. guttulata.* There was some doubt in McDunnough's mind (he is the Canadian Mayfly specialist) because the Spring Creek fly is somewhat larger than that found on other streams; however, he took the matter up with Speith and Needham, and the consensus of opinion was that it was the same fly, only somewhat larger. It is hard to tell if the flies on Spruce Creek and Stone Creek are the same species. I am convinced that it is possible to transplant different species on the same water and get hatches at different times—but the stream bed conditions should be the same. I should think that by the third year you will begin to see results, although in my case the flies started emerging about a week after they appeared on the parent stream, that is, three years plus one week to be exact.

"When I originally transplanted the Green Drakes in Middle Creek, I did it by the nymphs; that is, the nymphs were collected and transplanted, but the method was wrong. Many of them were injured in collecting, and it was too big a job to gather them in abundance. The successful program was accomplished by transferring the sub-imagoes in wire cages to the stream, and then liberating them. The fly now comes on yearly in abundance, although I don't believe there was more than 2500 in the original stocking. The ratio of females to males was about three to one, and the following evening after liberating them the spinners were observed laying their eggs naturally on the water."

Contents of a letter from Edward R. Hewitt, dean of American trout anglers and author of *Telling On The Trout:*

"Your mayfly stocking will probably succed to some extent, but you did not adopt the best method. This transfer of mayflies is very common in England, where the hatch is quite often all killed out from a stream or a section of stream by bad rainy weather when the flies are in the bushes changing their skins. If rain occurs then, they all perish. Mr. Lunn, the Keeper at the Houghton Club on the Test, worked out the best method of transferring mayflies, which is in regular use in England. He catches the flies about to lay eggs and puts them under a wire cover such as is used to keep off flies in restaurants and puts the cover over a china plate which contains water. When the eggs are laid he stacks the plates one over the other, with a strip of board in between them to keep them apart. The stack is taken to the place to be stocked and the plate placed on the bottom of the brook in a suitable place. They should be well scattered so as to get good distribution. When the eggs are hatched the plates are recovered. This method is completely successful.

"While the mayfly makes a very short time of very good fishing, it does not furnish any food for the trout during the rest of the year, and when the mayfly hatch is over the trout are stuffed and won't take surface flies well for some time. It has the advantage of bringing up the big trout to a fly better than other flies. They have a whole series of flies in English chalk streams, which hatch all during the season and provide good dry fly fishing all the year. I have arranged with Lunn to ship over a large number of the eggs of these flies for the Castilia stream in Ohio. They will arrive next June. The Castilia stream is very similar to the Test in water and in vegetation, and I am sure these flies will do well there.

"The mayfly is very variable in streams. It will exist for many years in a stream and then die out entirely, probably due to the weather killing the females. I have known many streams which had them at times and then they all disappeared. They can be reestablished by planting the eggs. The flies will hatch out at various times, from the same female; the flies will hatch in one, two, or three years from the same hatch of eggs. Lunn proved this in his aquarium. There are many families of mayflies. In some the nymphs can live in sandy bottom, in others in gravel, and in others in stony bottom. If the mayfly selected for planting is not suitable to the bottom the plant will be a failure. The bottoms of the streams must be similar when a transfer is to be made.

"In some streams the water conditions are such that every few years all the nymphs are killed out. This is true of any stream where the ice freezes on the bottom. I got mayflies started on the Neversink and they persisted for three years and then all were killed. This is why there are none on the Neversink. The conditions become impossible for them every few years. This may be true of the streams you are trying to stock. You may get them started and then they may all disappear in a few years. This is probably why they are not already in these streams. If your planting fails later on, don't be worried. You will then know that these streams have conditions at times unsuitable for mayflies. Only a few streams in this country will continually carry a mayfly population for many years at a time.

"The Willoweemoc above Livington Manor had the largest mayfly hatch I ever knew about fifty years ago. None have been seen there in twenty years now. They exist in the lower river but have never come back above. I don't know why.

"We don't know very much about the conditions which are suitable for the mayfly. These conditions must be suitable over the whole year and no one ever studies a stream for every day in the year and many years on end. It is quite likely that you will succeed in getting a mayfly hatch in streams where there are none now, but it is very doubtful if such a hatch will persist over many years in succession. If conditions were really suitable for mayflies they would already be there."

The practice was followed for at least two evenings of the hatch for each of the three following years, 1947 through 1949; and in each of these years distribution was made in four limestone streams of Cumberland County, Pennsylvania: Yellow Breeches Creek, Big Spring, the Letort and Cedar Run.

There were several refinements initiated after the two experiences of the first year. In order not to crowd the eggs more than necessary, several wash boilers were utilized instead of one. In addition to lining the boilers with cloth, small stones wrapped in cloth were placed on the bottom of each boiler, thus creating greater surface area and facilitating distribution. The boilers were three quarters filled with water so the eggs could adhere to a greater area of cloth.

Observation revealed that both the scuds and sow bugs (shrimp and cress bugs), which abound in limestone streams collected on the strips of cloth bearing the precious cargo; and the assumption was, that being carnivorous and scavengers, they were preying on the eggs. No doubt the crayfish in their nocturnal feeding activity did the same. To afford the utmost protection, the strips were placed in tubular containers made from hardware-cloth, the ends being stapled after insertion of the egg-laden cloth. These cages were then submerged in appropriate channels.

It is common belief that the Green Drake is in the nymph stage for three years. To bring about quickest and surest possibility for a sustained hatch, it was decided that the experiment should be carried on for at least three consecutive years at the same spots. (Actually it was conducted for three years under the most exacting scale possible, but the first year was charged to experience with the hope that some results were achieved.)

Much to our amazement the first emergence occurred the first year following the planting, proving that at least a few complete the metamorphose in one year. Probably others hatch in two years, something which could not be proved, and the predominant hatch taking place the third year—nature's method of perpetuation in the event of catastrophy.

Each season the spinners were netted between the 8th and 14th of June. Suprisingly, the duns and spinners observed on the stocked waters appeared between the 19th and 29th of May, indicating that the variation in temperature accelerated development.

As the years rolled along, no bonafide fishing hatch—either duns or spinners—of the Green Drake developed and during the seasons of '54 and '55 none at all were observed, although it is possible that some did emerge and return to deposit their eggs. The fact of the matter is that this hatch does not appear to have become acclimated to this environment, a really great disappointment. But the effort was not in vain. *Simulans*, the other big Mayfly which was netted at the same time, however in smaller quantity, is apparently here to stay and in quantity. *Simulans*, almost as large in size as *guttulata* and as interesting a hatch in every respect, has taken hold well on two of the four streams. It may have become established on the other two streams and may be emerging at the same time. Due to the fact that the interested individuals are capitalizing upon the resultant fishing hatch on two of the streams, they cannot be sure just what is transpiring in other parts over the same period of time.

The accepted imitation of the imago of *simulans* (now locally called Brown Drake) is a number 10 Adams with a canary yellow body. In one respect the fly has a tremendous advantage over the Green Drake: the fall of spinners sometimes settles on the water as early as 6:30 P. M. whereas *guttulata* usually holds back until dusk. One interesting aspect to date is the fact that as yet *simulans* has not spread over its normal span of time. Two evenings a year is the limit to date. The sub-imago must emerge at night, for very few duns have been observed on the water or leaving the water in spite of the fact that spinners occur in quantity.

Dr. Paul Needham is of the opinion that so long as there are a few remaining pairs of an aquatic insect in a watershed there is hope for the reestablishment of the hatch. Both *simulans* and *guttulata* may through the years become thoroughly entrenched in the limestone spring-streams of the Cumberland Valley. However, prospects for the former appear to be excellent, the chances of the latter, poor.

CHAPTER X

The Quill Gordon Fly

SO MUCH has been written about the Quill Gordon trout fly and its originator, Theodore Gordon, 1854-1915, that the writer hesitates to add anything more. However, so much confusion exists concerning the natural insect from which this famous fly was fashioned, that the writer feels the facts should be presented in order that one can form his own conclusions as to whether or not the fly was ever patterned after any specific insect.

Before delving into the theories concerning the natural insect, suppose we consider the dressing of the artificial. The writer has been unable to find any record of the dressing of the fly in John McDonald's *The Complete Fly Fisherman, The Notes and Letters of Theodore Gordon*. Neither has he been able to find an account of it in the old volumes of *Forests and Stream, The Fishing Gazette, Field and Stream* and *The American Angler*—publications which included among their contributors Theodore Gordon.

Perhaps the most authentic dressing of the fly is given in Harold H. Smedley's delightful little volume, *Fly Patterns and Their Origins*.

"For the Quill Gordon," he stated, "the wings should be a single upright bunch of wood duck barbules because the natural holds its wings erect and together when at rest which indicates a mayfly. Gordon called this fly a Blue Quill Gordon. The body was light peacock quill with a black edge. The hackle was dun or blue—whichever you wish—very light in color, almost transparent or the color of water. The body was wound with a very fine gold plated wire. Tails were three or four wisps from wood duck feathers."

The above description was probably secured from Roy Steenrod, Gordon's close personal friend and fishing companion. Please note the description of the hackle: *"dun or blue—whichever you wish—very light in color, almost transparent or the color of water."*

Dr. Edgar Burke in his book, *American Dry Flies and How to Tie Them* gives a very similar dressing for the fly, except that he substitutes barbules

117

from a dun cock's hackle for the tail instead of wood duck wisps. And so, down through the years the fly has been tied—always with dun or blue dun hackle.

And now getting back to the natural insect from which the fly may have been fashioned. From time to time the writer has received letters from various Pennsylvania anglers as to why no mention was made of the Quill Gordon in his book *Practical Fly Fishing*. Two of such letters I am quoting verbatim since they are typical examples of calling attention to the existing confusion:

Dear Mr. Wetzel:

A number of years ago I wrote you relative to a certain nymph question and you were very kind to reply. The information you gave me at that time has resulted in many pleasant hours of trout fishing.

Inasmuch as at the present time I am confronted with a perplexing problem, I am wondering if you would be good enough to give the information requested.

Over a period of years, I have accumulated quite a library of trout fishing books, including yours, Dr. Grove, Art Flick, E. R. Hewitt, Robert Salmon, Crowe and others, but your book, *Practical Fly Fishing* and Dr. Grove's *The Lure and Lore of Trout Fishing* are my two fishing bibles.

What I want to know is why there is so much importance placed on Quill Gordon, Light and Dark Hendrickson, Dry Red Quill and Cahill by most of these authors; they in turn giving the scientific name, showing approximate emergence dates, etc., without you even mentioning these flies in your list of naturals.

I feel that if they were of great importance to trout fishermen and are actually the naturals other authors claim they are, that you would have mentioned them in your book.

Our winter "round table" discussion goes something like this: "Well Wetzel is an authority on aquatic insect life, and if there were such flies, he certainly would have included them in his list of Pennsylvania insects that are important to the fly fishermen."

Would appreciate it very much if you could give me some logical explanation of this.

Very sincerely yours,
F. J. W.

Well, a letter like that puts a man on the spot, especially when they consider you an authority. Here's the other:

Dear Mr. Wetzel:

Maybe I'm over-booked and unlearned and shouldn't be writing this at all, but man to man there are a few items that are a bit beyond me and I have confidence in you to the extent of asking the why for.

Up until I tangled with the *Stream Side Guide* I was comparatively happy. You listed your wet flies and gave bell and book on the babies in your Emer-

The Quill Gordon Fly

gence Table. As I say I was happy. But the Devil has crept in. *Iron fraudator* and *Ephemerella sub-varia* aren't there. Neither is *Stenonema canadensis* and *ithaca* (and *cayuga*) and I am nonplussed. This is not to be taken as critical of your book; as long as I used the old crappers from Thaddeus Norris and Jim Leisenring I didn't suspect the fish were that way. Then my son let me into the club with a copy of *Practical Fly Fishing* by you know who, and I haven't been the same since. The trout haven't acted good either. Maybe Jim Leisenring got you to leave them out. He doesn't use them, he told me. Maybe you have legitimate reasons for omitting them as they might further complicate matters. You can see I am just groping around and have sort of fastened on to you as something substantial in a tottering world.

To identify myself, you were across the Brodheads one evening when I came up the stream and dared me to try for a breaking fish upstream from you —which I did—and finally hooked a fingerling on my dry *Stenonema canadensis* and *ithaca* size 13 in the Kitty Pool. I thought you were Pete Hidy. It was a tough day.

In case you find yourself in shape to put down a few thoughts, let yourself go. I'm trying to make up my so called mind about what I want to tie fresh for the coming year. What a sucker!

Yours truly,
G. S.

And now an open reply to the above letters:

The flies that I described in the entomological section of *Practical Fly Fishing* and the *Pennsylvania Angler* were all taken from the streams of Pennsylvania; they included: Kettle Creek, Pine Creek, Brodheads Creek, Young Womans Creek, First Fork of the Sinnemahoning, Lycoming Creek, Loyalsock Creek, Fishing Creek, Penns Creek, Middle Creek and many others, whereas the insects described by Preston J. Jennings in *A Book of Trout Flies* and Art Flick in *Stream-Side Guide to Naturals and Their Imitations* were in the main taken from New York waters.

I have never encountered *Stenonema cayuga,* and can find no record of it in *The Biology of Mayflies*. It apparently was so named after the monograph came out. Neither have I ever encountered *Stenonema canadense* (Light Cahill and *S. ithaca* on Pennsylvania waters. There is no record in the *Biology of Mayflies* of these insects being found in Pennsylvania, they being for the most part found in upper New York, Ontario, Quebec and other portions of Canada. This does not mean of course that they could not be in Pennsylvania. *Ephemerella sub-varia* and *E. invaria* (Hendrickson) are very similar, however, I have never found them in sufficient abundance on Pennsylvania waters to make up a dressing for them, although Charlie Fox advises that *sub-varia* is a wonderful early season hatch on the Yellow

Breeches and one of the four most important hatches of that stream. Needham lists these flies as being found in Hudson Bay, Ontario and Quebec, but has no record of them in Pennsylvania and New York according to *The Biology of Mayflies*. I have never found them farther south than Northern Pennsylvania and then only in sparse hatches, very scarce.

Jennings calls the Quill Gordon, *Iron pleuralis* and mentions that while he has no positive proof that it is the natural fly that Theodore Gordon copied, he is perfectly well satisfied that a well-tied Quill Gordon will be taken by the trout for this natural fly.

Flick calls the Quill Gordon, *Iron fraudator* and while he does not know whether or not this was the natural that Mr. Gordon copied, he is satisfied that the artificial Quill Gordon will take fish consistently when this Mayfly is on the water.

Needham, Traver and Hsu, *The Biology of Mayflies* state that *Iron fraudator* is so similar in general appearance to *Iron pleuralis* that they are unable to find any character other than genitalic structure by which to distinguish which is which. Further, the two species occur together; specimens of both have been taken in the same swarm.

From the above remark, one wonders whether or not the two specific flies might not be one and the same.

Now the present writer has discovered *Iron pleuralis* on many Pennsylvania streams. It is quite common and was taken April 20 on Brodheads Creek, April 16 on Young Womans Creek, June 5 on Fishing Creek and April 25 on Penns Creek. Year after year it appears on the above streams and usually within a week of the above recorded emergence dates. The female fly is conspicuous by a yellow ball of eggs attached to the tip of her abdomen. One can hardly drive along any of the above mentioned trout streams without having the windshield of the car spattered by the yellow egg sacs. You too have probably noticed it—sometimes they are so numerous as to make driving hazardous. Like all other Mayflies, the male is somewhat smaller than the female and resembles her except for the egg sac. This male fly I have described and pictured in *Practical Fly Fishing* and the *Pennsylvania Angler*. It is known as the Red Quill Spinner on Penns Creek, and I have kept that name. Now the reason it is called the Red Quill is that the body segments are a reddish brown corresponding to a red dyed peacock quill, and the legs are reddish brown also.

The dun or sub-imago stage of this fly (Jenning's and Flick's Quill Gordon) has a blood red body; the body segments are not so sharply differentiated like they are in the imago or spinner stage, and the legs and tail of the fly are reddish brown—not dun or blue dun corresponding to

The Quill Gordon Fly

the dressing of the Quill Gordon; the wings of the dun could conceivably be imitated by a wood ducks flank feather, but the hackle and body quill just do not agree. I have reared this fly from dun to spinner stage and the specimens were checked by Dr. McDunnough, the Canadian entomologist who specializes in Mayflies. I have never tried to describe the dressing for the sub-imago or dun stage heretofore.

Jennings and Flick are undoubtedly right that the Quill Gordon will take trout when *Iron pleuralis* or *I. fraudator* is over the water. I have great respect for their ability and judgment, but somehow or other I cannot believe that this was the insect that Gordon copied when he designed the famous Quill Gordon. Apparently some doubt must exist in their minds also, since neither are positive as to its being the fly.

The present writer believes that the Quill Gordon is not an imitation of any specific Mayfly, but that it embodies features copied possibly from three or four different insects; perhaps certain features of the artificial fly are purely fancy—I don't know. In view of the confusion that has existed, I felt it wise to deliberately not mention the Quill Gordon in *Practical Fly Fishing* and in the *Pennsylvania Angler*.

Perhaps Gordon too had his tongue in his cheek when he wrote in the Oct. 31, 1908 issue of the *Fishing Gazette:*

"I was amused recently when an angling friend informed me that the birds were taking many of the Quill Gordon flies in the air after they rose from the water. This reminds me of those large hatches of Pink Wickhams* which were reported by an observer some years ago.

Could it be that Gordon himself ridiculed the idea of the Quill Gordon having a prototype? The inference seems to suggest it; however, you be the judge.

* The Pink Wickham is a fancy variation of Wickhams Fancy and is attributed to the famous fly tyer George Holland, who changed the wings to pink landrail.

CHAPTER XI

Fishing the Wet Fly

AFTER REVIEWING old American angling literature, the writer was struck with the scarcity of information on how to fish a wet fly for trout. In the usual case, one or two cursory sentences described the art, but in general everything else seems to be covered except the actual technique of how to do it. Here and there one reads about working the fly in a fancy and erratic manner; however, such methods are unnecessary, unproductive, and usually scare more fish than they attract. In general they are written to impress the novice. How well they have done that can be seen on almost any of our trout streams today. Some of the fancy methods now in use are spectacular and highly impressive to the tyro, but they do not catch fish.

The writer fished the wet fly when a boy and at a time when dry flies were unknown. Then the dry fly made its appearance and the old reliable wet flies were put on the shelf for a period of almost twenty years. After the fascination of dry fly fishing wore off, the old time wet flies were again tried and with such success that he has employed them in most of his trouting during the past ten years. There's no mystery about wet fly fishing and no need of working the fly in a fancy manner, as advocated by some writers. The method used is essentially the same as that in vogue when I was a boy, except that a few slight improvements have crept in over the years. The method is known as the natural drift.

Before getting into the matter of how to fish the fly, let's look into a few of the slight improvements that have developed.

First of all the contemporary wet flies are now tied with ringed eyes only and do not have the looped snell so commonly used years ago. Two and three wet flies are still in vogue; however, the leader is now tied with short droppers, which replace the old loops formerly used. The method of incorporating the dropper with the leader is shown in the sketch. It's not difficult to tie such a leader—the knots are still the old timers, except that one end is somewhat longer than the other when tying together the two sections of

124   *Trout Flies—Naturals and Imitations*

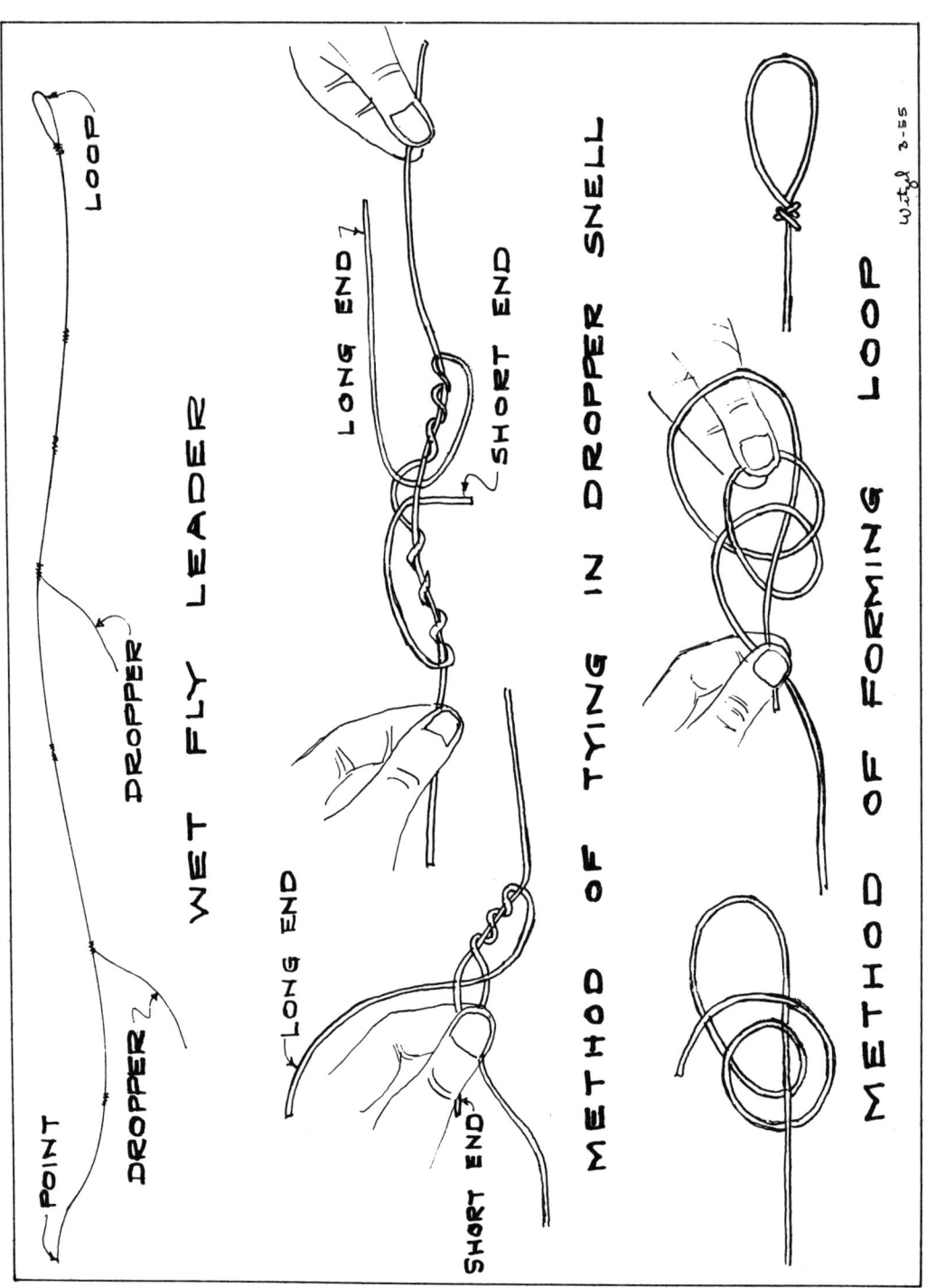

PLATE XXIX.

gut or nylon; this long end serves as the dropper and replaces the old time snell. I have never seen this method in print before, and it is a definite improvement over the old bulky, bubble catching looped leader. Its invention can be attributed to my friend Mel Wood. After the snell becomes shortened it is a simple matter to tie in a new dropper.

I personally do not change flies a great deal while on the stream. My casts are usually made up beforehand, and I have a lot of them prepared and individually housed in cellophane envelopes. This method is particularly good for people with poor eyesight, for trying to thread a fly when trout are breaking all around one can be particularly exasperating.

The flies have not changed too radically over the years. The form is still the same—a few new types have crept in—however, the main difference is in the matter of color. The old gaudy wet flies have been replaced with those of more somber hue, in keeping with the natural trout stream insects. The new, sober colored flies came into vogue shortly after the brown trout was introduced in this country. These fish proved to be highly discriminating feeders, and unlike the brook trout, they just weren't going to be taken in by such gaudy creations as Parmacheenee Belles, Silver Doctors, and the like.

And now let's get on to fishing the fly. Two methods are in common use; one for slow water, the other for swift. Both utilize the old time natural drift principle.

Fishing the Wet Fly in Swift Water

Fish downstream, casting your flies slightly farther down than directly across the current. If the water is very swift, check your cast in mid air so that the flies flutter down on the water with a lot of slack line. The principle is exactly the same as that employed by the dry fly fisherman when he seeks to avoid drag. The slack line will permit the flies to sink quickly, deep down into the water. I prefer this method to an upstream cast since slack will be more quickly taken out of the line, thereby achieving better control.

Now let the flies drift downstream naturally with the current. Impart no motion whatsoever, but follow with your rod tip the course of the flies as they tumble downstream.

Following the flies with the rod tip should probably be elaborated. The rod is constantly held high in a position comparable to eleven o'clock; and the movement in following the flies is so slow and slight as to be scarcely imperceptible. When you judge that the flies are over a locality where a trout may be hiding, the downstream course of the rod tip is stopped; the swift water striking the stationary line causes it to become taut, and the flies—acting very much alive—are then pulled upwards towards the surface. The trout hits the fly at this time or a little later, when the leader is straightening out. There are a lot of good wet fly fishermen who complete the drift, that is, they do not stop the rod and bring the flies to the surface until the leader has straightened out directly below where they are standing; then again, there are others who bring the flies to the surface two and three times before the drift is completed. In all cases, hold the flies taut and stationary for at least twenty seconds before lifting them from the water for the next cast. It is surprising how many trout take the fly after it has straightened out and is waving back and forth laterally in the current.

Unlike in slow water fishing, one is hardly ever in doubt when a trout hits the fly; they do it with a slashing strike that is really something to feel. One seldom notices the fish take the fly because it is sunk so deeply. Many anglers breaking into the wet fly game get plenty of strikes but hook few fish. This is caused by not holding the rod tip high enough in the air. Keep it always at the eleven o'clock angle; and then when a trout hits the fly there will be enough spring in the rod that the hook will be automatically set. Another reason for not hooking trout and holding them can be blamed on heavy striking. Trout hit the wet fly so hard that instinctively one sets the hook with a sharp hard jerk tearing the fly from their mouth. This is definitely wrong and can only be corrected by exercising self control. Learn to hook the trout by a mere turn of the wrist; if this is not possible, then get the softest action fly rod procurable—one that bends easily down to the grip

Fishing the Wet Fly in Slow Water

Trout can be caught with the wet fly in slow water using the method described above; however, a much more successful way is the following: fish upstream, similar to that shown in the sketch. The dropper fly should be a bushy affair—one that floats well, such as a Bi-visible. Trout will be taken on this; however, its main function is that of a float, since it registers when a trout takes the point or submerged wet fly.

In slow moving water, trout take up a position where the current carries the greatest number of insects. Here they lie, a foot or so under the surface, and they rarely move from this location; they move upwards only to take the floating flies carried down on the surface, and to right and left when they take a nymph or submerged wet fly carried by the current. In this position the trout's movements are deliberate and unhurried and he rarely moves more than a foot from this location when taking his food. Neither does he hit it with a bang and run away with it, as is the case with

Fishing the Wet Fly

a trout in swift water, but he swallows it, or spits it out if not to his liking, with an almost imperceptible movement.

To verify this, watch some of the trout feeding in slow water at Fishermen's Paradise on Spring Creek. Drift your wet flies over them in the usual downstream cast and nothing apparently happens; yet if one watches closely one can see the trout move slowly to right or left and take the fly, spitting it out—and all with a movement so slight that it is not recognized.

Now get below the fish. Cast your flies upstream and retrieve the slack line with your left hand similar to dry fly fishing. Keep your eye on the Bi-visible bobber; as it comes floating downstream watch when it stops or starts moving in another direction—then strike!

The method is highly productive. To try it is to be convinced.

CHAPTER XII

Fishing the Dry Fly

DRY FLY fishing is considered by many as the highest pinnacle of the art; however, the writer feels that wet fly and nymph fishing are equally as important, perhaps more so. For more than twenty years I fished the dry fly exclusively, and I learned many things.

For instance, trout taken by the dry fly are in general smaller than those taken on nymphs and wet flies; this does not apply, however, to the hatch of the big Mayfly, at which time the old lunkers feed ravenously on the surface.

It is also a misconception that a surface feeding fish can only be taken on a dry fly. Nothing is farther from the truth. A finished wet fly angler will take as many surface feeding trout as can be caught on the dry fly.

Perhaps the most fascinating part of dry fly fishing is that the trout are always seen as they rise to take the artificial. Some of the rises are spectacular, others are mere dimples on the surface, but all in all, there's a thrill attached to either kind that is hard to describe.

Trout always lie with their heads upstream, usually on the alert for any food that may be carried down by the current. The surface feeding fish takes up a position near the top of the water, usually at a spot where the current constricts and diverts all surface food into channel-like confines. Here, at the edge of swift moving water, he lies, constantly scanning the surface for any insects which are carried downstream.

The dry fly fisherman takes advantage of his position; that is, he fishes upstream so that he will be unobserved by the trout; he also studies the location of the currents so that his artificial may ride naturally downstream, uninfluenced by drag. Drag is that particular thing that causes a dry fly to skitter across the water instead of floating naturally downstream; it is usually caused by a swifter intervening current striking the line or leader and pulling the floating fly rapidly along with it.

Only one fly is used in dry fly fishing, and the big problem is to keep it dry so that it will float. Some anglers do this entirely by false casting; that is, the fly is cast back and forth in the air without it touching the water, and the moisture is removed in this way; others—the great majority—use a combination of false casting and annointing the fly with some floating preparation such as deer fat, Silicone, or Mucilin. To prevent shadows from falling on the water and frightening the fish, the leader should sink below the surface. The application of soap, mud, or glycerine will facilitate this sinking. The line should also be thoroughly greased to insure its floating. Here again, false casting facilitates the floating of the line.

Various methods are in use to prevent drag, the most common being the slack line cast. This is accomplished by checking the cast in the air at a time when the fly is on its forward journey over the surface. The fly will then flutter lightly to the surface, carrying with it coils of loose slack line and leader. If the loose slack line or leader falls in the swift intervening current, it will be carried downstream some distance before it straightens out and starts pulling the fly. That briefly is the problem. Try to keep the dry fly floating naturally over the best places.

As the line and leader float downstream, reach forward with the free left hand and strip in line, holding it in coils. Taking up the slack line must be done carefully so as to avoid drag, and only enough should be taken up to insure setting the hook in the fish. If a trout has not taken the fly, it will keep floating downstream until eventually drag sets in. When this occurs, it should be picked up, a number of false casts made to eliminate the moisture, and at the critical moment the coils of line held in the left hand will be released or shot. The cast will again be checked when it is judged that the fly is over the fish and the loose falling line over the swift intervening current.

Other methods of preventing drag are by means of the Right and Left Hooks or curve casts. The Right Hook is made as follows: in a horizontal plane parallel with the water make a few false casts, stripping off line with the left hand until the required estimated distance is out. Check the final cast when the forward motion is about three-fourths completed, so that the large loop in the line and leader will not have an opportunity of straightening out. The line and leader will now lie on the surface extended in a curve or hook; and if the cast has been successfully made the bend of it will be located more or less symmetrically about the center of the swift water. The current in its downstream course puts a belly in the upstream bent line, but it will travel quite some distance before artificial impetus is imparted to the fly.

The Left Hook is performed exactly as above, except that the angler must place himself in the position of a left handed caster; that is, the casting

Fishing the Dry Fly

will be done with the right arm crossed over the left shoulder, all work being done as before in a horizontal plane parallel with the water.

I have often wondered whether or not we might be going too deeply into this matter of drag. Last year on Spring Creek I had a regular field day, catching and releasing almost a hundred large trout. These fish were all taken in the slower moving pools by a combined wet and dry fly method. The fly, a No. 6 long shanked hook, Palmer, tied with closely spaced yellow hackle, was jerked slightly as it floated downstream. When a trout was noticed following it, the fly was given a quick jerk, which pulled it under the water. Invariably the fly was taken with a great splash just as it was going under water.

One also wonders about the effectiveness of the Spiders or long hackled flies as they are skittered or skated across the surface. This resembles drag very much, except that a pause is made between jerks, which after all is somewhat different from the continuous pull on a fly once drag sets in.

CHAPTER XIII

Fishing the Nymph

IN THE chapter entitled NYMPHS we have learned how the immature stages of insects live and behave. This information is important and vital especially now, when it is to be put to practical use in fishing the artificial nymph.

Trout feed on nymphs the year around and we are fishing with an imitation of their most common food. Naturally the imitation must bear a close resemblance to the natural or the trout will not take it. The imitation must also be worked or fished in a method corresponding to that affected by the natural, and the depth where it is to be fished must be within the range of the trouts vision. The above are the three basic fundamentals.

Nymph fishing is easy to learn and the method proves most productive when the streams are low and clear. Earlier in the season the other underwater method, wet fly fishing, will perhaps prove more effective.

In nymph fishing, one fly or nymph only is used and the best success is obtained with a long, fine leader tapered to 5X. When the trout are in deep water the leader should be weighted with lead wire or split shot so that the nymph can be worked near the bottom. This is the locality where trout lie because the water is coldest there. When the water is warm and the sun is hot and bright, trout also lie near the bottom in the swift, deep and heavy riffles. When they are lying there, nothing will induce them to rise, therefore we must go down after them.

Fish upstream in much the same manner as that affected by the worm fishermen. Let the nymph come tumbling downstream over the rocks and when it gets below you, bring it up towards the surface. You will become snagged often and lose many flies, however, you will also catch fish which you cannot do by other methods. As the fly comes tumbling downstream, retrieve line with the left hand, and retrieve it slightly faster than the current is carrying the fly; in short, endeavor to create a mild form of drag. The purpose of this is to quickly sense when the fish hits the fly.

To achieve the same result as the above, many anglers use a small bi-visible dry fly attached a few feet above the nymph which serves as a float and warning when the trout seizes the artificial. What is most important is keenness of perception, since in the majority of cases trout seize and spit out the fly without your being aware of it. Fishing nymphs deep down in the water requires a great amount of skill. Cultivate the method, for the majority of large trout stay in such water.

A successful nymph fisherman presents the fly to the fish at the proper depth and in the localities they frequent. Around early May the trout desert the deep flat-water holes and take up positions in the shallower riffles. Should a violent storm occur which raises the creek level, the trout get out of the heavy water and take up positions in the eddies along the stream banks. As the water recedes, they again resume their position in the riffles. Around the latter part of May as the days grow warmer and the water gets hotter and shallower, the trout begin to find a scarcity of cover and oxygen in their former homes on the shallow riffles. They now begin to congregate in the heavier, greenish, white-water riffles, lying deep down during the heat of day and cruising back and forth in the white water during early mornings and late evenings. If there is still not sufficient aeration and coolness, the trout wait for the first high water when they begin their upstream migration to the cold water feeder streams. The above applies particularly to the brook trout, to a somewhat lesser extent to the brown trout, and not at all to the rainbow trout in the east.

But getting back to fishing. As the nymphs are rising to the surface to transform into the winged fly, another method of procedure is desirable. Cast directly upstream, allow a few moments for the nymph to sink, then gradually start it working downstream and up to the surface by means of a few short jerks. Trout as a rule follow its downstream journey and often seize it just at the surface when the artificial is being lifted off the water for the next cast. This type of angling is most successful when the Mayfly sub-imagoes are rising from the not too swift current.

Large trout—and by that I mean really large—like to take cover in deep flat-water pools. Dams seem to be favorite lurking places, especially those where the water is so deep that one cannot see bottom. Such big fish are often taken with nymphs using the following technique. Allow the heavily weighted fly to settle down on the bottom. Permit it to lie there and occasionally take in a few inches of line with the left hand. Repeat the procedure and, above all, do not be in a hurry. Many a big trout has been taken which struck the nymph when it was lying still, or after it had been moved slightly on the bottom.

Fishing the Nymph

In the swift water, a still different method of procedure is used. This is one of my favorite casts and is made diagonally downstream. Many will say that it is a modification of wet fly fishing, however, I have found very little difference between fishing the wet fly and the nymph—all are underwater methods. As the natural nymph comes tumbling downstream with the current it usually endeavors to get into the quieter water where transformation to the winged fly occurs. It also happens that occasionally nymphs become dislodged by the current and float downstream, there to obtain a new foothold where the water is not so swift. Here the cast should be made diagonally downstream directly in the center of the white water. Throw slack line in the cast (same as in dry fly fishing) so that the nymph will sink before the line starts straightening out and pulling it into the quieter side water. I cannot emphasize too much the importance of shooting the slack line. This is perhaps the greatest asset of them all, for one must try different levels to determine where the trout are located. I usually fish so deeply that I never see the flash of the fish. All that is noticeable is a vicious tug, a really vicious tug. Two seconds after the trout is splashing around on top of the water, and then the battle really starts!

When trout are feeding on nymphs, certain indications manifest themselves. Whenever an upheaval occurs just underneath the surface of the water, trout are bulging; that is, they are actively engaged in snapping up the nymphs swimming to the top of the water to split open the nymphal skin and emerge as winged flies. Occasionally fish feeding this way will follow a nymph to the surface, and if the winged fly should just at that moment escape from the shuck, the trout will rise and take it. Also, when trout are bulging, one can often get a glimpse of a tail fin protruding above the surface of the water. Trout literally stand on their heads when nymphs rise to the surface.

Another good indication that trout are nymphing can be obtained from the streaks that follow in the wake of fish as they swirl about, feeding avidly on the pupa of midges which are hanging vertically at the surface waiting for the pupal skin to split open. This is more noticeable on the quiet placid pools and is at times a scene of great activity, for the trout feed ravenously on the practically quiescent pupae if knowing the midges will soon emerge and fly away.

Still another indication—perhaps one that escapes observation nine times out of ten—is the fish which lie near the surface close to a lazy riffle and which do not move in their feeding activity more than a foot from such locations. When they take up such a position it is usually at a time when the nymphs, in flushes, are trying to get into the quieter side water. Such fish are feeding constantly, and since so many nymphs are carried by, it is unnecessary for the trout to move or dart about. Now and then they may be seen moving a few inches to right or left, sucking in the nymphs and occasionally spitting out some particle which was mistaken for food. When so engaged, such fish are extremely hard to catch, mainly because it is difficult to sense when they have taken the fly.

Be constantly experimenting. Trout feed on nymphs the year 'round and there is still much to be learned in this type of angling. Unlike dry fly fishing, you need not wait for the natural fly to be abroad, but can venture forth with strong hope of success even in the coldest snow-water.

CHAPTER XIV

Pages From The Diary

FOR A great many years I have been keeping a diary of my fishing trips, and the following accounts appear exactly as written. I have picked out these entries which I thought to be most interesting, without regard to the year, but the dates of the month are in all cases given.

* * * *

April 13—Spent the evening tying Red Quill nymphs and wet flies—also a few Little Black Stone flies. Tomorrow night I am going home to fish with Dad on the opening day and the Red Quill should prove A-1. Last year I took 9 trout on Young Woman's Creek with the Red Quill, and I'm hoping to duplicate that performance on the 15th.

April 15—Dad and I fished Swift Run above Troxelville today. Weather very cold with occasional snow flurries. Stream very high. A few Little Black Caddis Flies over the water but the Red Quill was absent. Fell in. After wringing out my clothes I was unable to get back into them as they froze stiff. Walked back to car naked carrying clothes in hand. Dad, who had also fallen in was already in car with heater going strong. No trout taken.

April 15—Fished Cedar Run today. Cold. No trout rising and none taken.

April 15—Clark Kepner, his son Allen, and I, fished the Yellow Breeches at Huntsdale, also Big Spring at Newville. Water temperature 45° F. and trout sluggish. Only saw three fish taken all morning and those on worms. In the afternoon, Kep and I went to Fishing Creek, where we caught three trout. The Little Black Caddis and Red Quill were out in fairly good numbers and their imitations were responsible for the fish mentioned above. Fished wet fly, using the Red Quill on the point.

April 16—Warren Jones and I went up to the Split Rock Club today and fished both the Stretch and the Dream Mile. The Little Black Stonefly was over the water in good numbers, and above the bridge over the Tobyhanna (Dream Mile) I took four nice brown trout on its imitation. Warren also took four nice fish.

April 16—This evening while walking home from Penns Creek I counted 35 deer grazing in my fields. Fishing was wonderful. Red Quill over the water and trout were taking the fly on the surface. Stream low and clear and weather warm and cloudy; ideal for trout fishing. Kept eight fish ranging from 10 to 14 inches. Lost track of the number of trout caught.

April 18—Took a 15-inch brook trout in the Spinning Wheel Hole at my farm on Penns Creek. Fish taken on a Red Quill fished deep. Trout heavy and well conditioned. Sure am pleased as such brookies are very scarce. Deer browsing everywhere.

April 20—Took a 17-inch brown trout on Kettle Creek today. Fish caught on a Black Ant wet fly. This was a good christening for my new three ounce Winston fly rod. Stream high and running wild. Fell in at the Cannonading Hole and lost quite a bit of tackle.

April 23—Mel Wood, Dick Day, George Richards, and myself fished Herman Bergdorf's water on the Brodheads today. Took 7 trout—all brook trout but one, which was a brown—on the Red Quill female with her yellow egg sack. Fished wet. Very peculiar that trout would not take the Back Ant dropper fly. The Black Ant is one of the best flies on the creek and nearly always takes fish.

April 24—Fished Brodheads Creek today with same group. Took four nice brown trout on the Black Ant. Fish around 14 inches long. All were taken in the big pool, where Wood fell in a few years before. Met our old fishing friends Mr. Schrader and Mr. Acuff, who are usually here over every weekend.

April 25—Fished Young Woman's Creek today. Cold. Nothing but experience.

April 28—Fished White Clay Creek with Reg. Ellis today. No trout taken.

April 29—Clark Kepner, Manley White, Ralph Endriss, George Richards, and Kepner's son fished the Yellow Breeches and Boiling Springs today. Result of trip 4 trout. Water in good condition but fish not rising. Met Charlie Fox and Bob McCafferty, who reported fishing poor.

April 30—Dad and I fished the North Branch of Middle Creek today. Weather rather cold with rain in the morning, but towards noon the Red Legged March Flies were everywhere struggling on the surface of the water.

Pages from the Diary

These flies belong to the family *Bibionidae*, genus *Bibio* and apparently do not rise from the water, since I have seen them crawling out of small holes on the clay banks of the stream. Having no monograph I am unable to identify them as to species, so am sending a few to Mr. Cresson of the Academy of Natural Sciences in Philadelphia. Took five nice trout on the imitation of this fly, which I tied along the streamside. When opened, the stomach contents of these fish revealed an amazing quantity of these flies. (Note added later bearing no date) "Mr. Cresson advised that these flies were *Bibio femoratus*."

May 1—George T. Richards and I fished the Yellow Breeches with Bob McCafferty and Charlie Fox. No trout taken, everyone being more content to lay along the stream bank and discuss fishing and fly life.

May 1—Jack Fetterholf and I fished the North Branch of Middle Creek today. No luck, yet there was an abundance of flies over the water. Hundreds of Light Stone flies and Alder Flies were congregated on the concrete bridge; and in the eddies the Red Legged March Fly was still struggling on the surface. Today the trout would not take the imitation. Fished wet and dry flies with no success, but late in the afternoon I turned over a nice trout using a quill nymph. Apparently he was hooked deeply, for he would not come again.

May 2—Fished Penns Creek above Cherry Run today. Extremely heavy hatch of small caddis flies congregated on large rock which protruded above water. Rested awhile on rock and watched them skimming over the surface and descending beneath the water at edge of rock. Flies had smoky colored wings, about one-fourth of an inch long and had black bodies. Secured a number and submitted them to Mr. Cresson in Philadelphia. No trout taken, only two rises being observed all day. (Note added later ("Mr. Cresson unable to identify the caddis flies."

May 3—Fished Fishing Creek in Lancaster County all day. Very hot and no trout feeding. Caught one small brown trout on a Fan Wing Royal Coachman just before dark. A few small, brownish black caddis flies skimming over the water, similar to those on Penns Creek last year. Fishing never good when these flies are on the water.

May 6—Fished the Lackawaxen today with Jack Frost, Owen Gay, Henry Gunther, Court Steelman, and Bill Moore and stayed at Owen's camp on Little Spruce Lake. Took one rainbow trout and lost two others in same pool; one tore off a Black Ant and the other, a larger fish, ran away with the leader and three flies.

May 7—Bob Curtin, George Richards, and I fished Penns Creek today. Creek slightly high, weather warm, and lots of flies (Black Quills) over the water. Fished wet and took six trout on the Black Quill. Fished from Cortons down to Hironomus and stayed at Elmer Kahley's. Very tired. Unable to cross creek due to high water. Farther downstream I came to a wire across the creek and watched a young boy inch his way across. He stated that it was easy so I tried it. When about half way over, the wires started moving back and forth, and looking down into the swift, rushing water twenty feet below, I wished I was anywhere else. Luckily I made it, but no more wire rope walking for me.

May 8—Same group fished same stream. George and I started in above wire across creek, and in the deep riffle above the bend I tied into a trout that took almost all my line off the reel. George was watching the fun from the bank. Ran him around for a few minutes—rather he ran me around—then the fish tore off the Early Brown Spinner and departed.

May 9—Fished Queens Run today and took six trout on the Black Ant.

May 13—Bob Curtin and I left this evening for the Brodheads. Put up at Erick's Hotel Rapids, along railroad at Analomink. Got awake at night and thought train was coming through bedroom.

May 14—Took three rainbow trout on the Brodheads, fishing wet fly. Ran across my old friend Jim Leisenring, who had just lost a large trout. Jim presented me with a duplicate of the fly the big trout tore off. Chatted awhile; then we went back to the hotel and drank beer and talked fishing. Jim still very active despite his age.

May 15—Fished Spring Creek today. The small crane fly known as the Yellow Spider was on the water, but today few fish were rising to it. Returned to the water two trout and kept two, one of which was plump and well conditioned. Met Bob McCafferty and Alex Sweigart on the stream. Cold and rainy.

May 16—George Richards, Bob Hall, the outdoor writer, Mel Wood, and I fished Herman Burgdorf's water on the Brodheads today. Few fish taken and few flies abroad. A swallow flying low over the water picked Wood's dry fly off the surface and we had quite a time releasing it. Down to Charlie Rethoret's (Analomink Charlie) hotel in the evening, where we drank beer and were entertained by Charlie's guests, a group of rabid fly fishers, among whom was the angling poet Don Brooks. Charlie couldn't do enough for us, his hospitality was unbounded. Food was rationed, but we ate his few remaining saindwiches and drank his scotch and everybody got about half high. Don Brooks sat down at the bar and dashed off a poem entitled "Reconversion," which he autographed and presented to me. (Note added later) "The poem was later published in the *Pennsylvania Angler*."

Pages from the Diary

May 17—Came to Penns Creek for the week, staying at Elmer Kahley's. Today I had hold of the same large trout I lost two weeks ago. Can't seem to land this fish. Caught two trout, each about a foot long, on the Yellow Body Grey Hackle.

May 18—A caddis fly with a green egg sack over Penns Creek today. Took two trout on a streamside constructed pattern of it. Fished till dark, and while coming out of the woods I ran a brush in my eye. Spent a miserable night.

May 19—Went down to Mifflinburg to the doctor, who fixed up my eye. Fished down around Glen Iron and took a nice 15 inch fish. In the evening Kahley's son and I went to DeLugi's, where I took a 14 inch brown trout on the Black Ant.

May 20—Went to Spring Creek this morning. Hundreds of fishermen. Fished only an hour and took five trout. Kept one 18 inches long—then back to Penns Creek. In the evening attended a square dance at the Union County Sportsmen's Club.

May 20—Stayed last night at Al Goodlander's camp on Little Weikert Run. Fished Penns Creek from Cherry Run upstream towards the Paddy Mountain Tunnel. Weather warm and cloudy, with occasional showers; ideal for dry fly fishing. The Black Quill, Pale Evening Dun, and March Brown were all out in good numbers and the trout were rising well. Noticed some Alder Flies and Yellow Spiders which were still unexpectedly abroad. Took eight fish, five on the Pale Evening Dun and three on the Black Quill, the largest being 14 inches. About a mile below the tunnel I tied into a monstrous brown trout, which ended with the fish swimming away with my Black Quill and part of the leader. Fried fish at the hunting cabin and again stayed there overnight. Saw four deer.

May 20—Fished Swift Run and caught five nice trout. About a quarter of a mile below Aumiller's Dam I took a 15 inch brown trout on a Yellow Spider just as it was growing dark. The fish put up quite a scrap, and when I hit him on the head he disgorged an eight inch brook trout. Pale Evening Duns beginning to come on the water.

May 20—Fished Weikert Run this morning. Counted eight partially decomposed deer (lying along the water) that had starved during last winter's heavy snow. The natives say that during heavy snows the deer eat laurel, drink at the creek, get bloated, and then die. Noticed the Dark Green Drake, a Mayfly that afterwards turns into the Brown Drake, was just emerging from the water. The trout had not yet become accustomed to it and were not rising.

Returned to the water four small brown trout taken on the Black Quill. Then drove over to Spring Creek. Caught eight trout and kept two, which I gave to my cousin, Sammy Wetzel of Sunbury, whom I chanced to meet.

May 20—About 10:00 A. M. I caught two large brown trout in Middle Creek on a specially designed streamer fly. This fly, about five inches long, and tied on a No. 1 long shanked hook, had a yellow chenille body, yellow marabou wings, red wool tail, and scarlet hackle. The fish were caught in the large pool to the left of Grimm's Dam, looking downstream. One fish was 19 and the other 21 inches.

May 21—Raised another large trout in the same pool at Grimm's Dam but nicked him pretty hard. He would not come again. Left for home. Caught a total of 28 trout during the week, 18 brown and 10 brook.

May 21—Fished Kettle Creek today with Kenneth Wykoff and caught one brook trout and one fallfish. In the afternoon, drove to Beavertown to visit Dad. Went fishing in Middle Creek, and in the evening ran into an enormous hatch of the Pale Evening Spinners. All were females, and the windshield of the car was completely covered with yellow egg sacks. In a distance of less than a mile I had to stop the car three times to wipe off the glass, driving being dangerous. These flies were lost. At some places they were as much as a quarter of a mile away from the water and apparently could not locate the stream due to the heavy rain and wind. Believe that they mistook the black macadam road for the creek, since they were rising and falling directly above it. Query—Will these flies be on the water in future years?

May 21—Warren Jones and I left this evening for the Little Lehigh. Put up at the Clifton Hotel. Took a couple of small trout before dark. Few flies on water.

May 22—Fished a few hours early this morning on Weiker Run. Saw three deer just as it was growing daylight, one of them scaring me almost to death by whistling no more than ten feet away. Caught one brown and one native trout. Lots of flies over the water and trout feeding for a short time on surface. Water crystal clear, and almost impossible to get close enough to the pools without frightening the fish. Very peculiar fly on the water: black antennae; yellow body sprinkled with red dots; two short tails and two pairs of hyaline wings, both pairs of same length.

May 23—Left this morning for the Beaverkill. Stopped off at Harry Darbee's and went with him down to Walt Dette's to get a New York State

Pages from the Diary

fishing license. Darbee wanted me to stay at his house and promised to go fishing with me in the morning. Spent a very pleasant evening with the Darbee's, both of whom are renowned fly tyers.

May 24—Instead of fishing the Beaverkill, Darbee and I drove over to the river, where he had been taking some nice trout. I caught one 17 inches long and two others 12 inches, the latter which I returned to the water. Harry took a 20 inch brown and one of 12 inches on a Black Ghost worked deeply in a heavy riffle. Took my fish on a large Black Ant tied on a No. 4 hook.

May 25—Ben Baird, Harold Baird, Ray Heckman, Mort Parker, and I fished Little Pine Creek today. Took a 16 inch brown trout on a Yellow Marabou Streamer, then went upstream to the Block House. No more trout taken until late in the afternoon. Was ready to quit when going downstream to the car I encountered Heckman who informed me that he had taken the limit of ten trout during the past hour on wet flies. The fish were rising to Ginger Quill Duns, *Stenonema fuscum,* which had lately appeared on the water. Proceeding below him about a quarter of a mile, where the hatch was thickest, I immediately began to take trout on the dry fly imitation. Took 10 trout during the next half hour, then quit fishing.

May 26—Weather hot and muggy. Spent the forenoon on Fishing Creek in Sullivan County. No sign of fly life abroad but apparently the Brown Quill was hatching, since many cracked and empty nymphal skins came floating down with the current. Underneath the covered bridge below Benton I tried to interest an old lunker with all kinds of flies, nymphs, streamers, and bucktails but he would have none of them. No fish rising anywhere, so drove over to Spring Creek. Chatted for a time with Art Snyder, the warden, and my old friend Jake Knisely at the Paradise. They informed me that the Shad Fly was well under way. Wandered out to the stream and encountered Dutch Derr. Dutch and I fished together the remainder of the day. No flies abroad and few fish rising. About 15 minutes before dark the Shad Fly (Grey and Black Drakes) came on in great numbers and the trout simply went wild. The Grey Drake seems to be the favorite fly of the trout, no doubt because she is filled with eggs up to her head. I noticed that these eggs protrude from the underside of her abdomen like two small tubes. Everyone was catching trout. Leaders were torn off like so much thread, and due to feeding fish, the surface of the water resembled a boiling cauldron. Checked out with two trout, 18 and 19 inches, just before the whistle sounded. Went down below the project to clean the fish and had to brush away a three inch scum of spent flies before I could wash off the fish.

May 27—Expected to have wonderful sport tonight on Spring Creek, but in the evening just before the Shad Fly came on, the creek turned muddy. Big hatch but the trout never knew it.

May 27—Heavy rains all week so decided to fish White Deer Creek today. Water high but not too discolored. Took a 16 inch brown trout on a Ginger Quill. While attempting to cross the creek, I was swept downstream for about thirty feet. Lost my wading staff, fly book, and other tackle.

May 27—George Richards and I fished Spring Creek today. In the evening the Shad Fly came on in good numbers and we had wonderful sport. Took 8 large trout on the Grey Drake fanwing. Stayed at the Brockerhoff Hotel. In the evening, while drinking beer, a group of State College boys came in. They stayed there all evening and got about half high. Towards closing time their leader came over to our table and demanded:

"Are you for me or against me?"

"Why I'm for you, of course," I replied.

"Well," he said, "just remember that. If anything starts around here, don't forget which side you're on." Nothing started.

May 27—Went up to the Split Rock Club and took my son Bill along as my guest. Fished the Stretch (Tunkhannock Creek) near the lower end where it flows into Tobyhanna Creek. Ginger Quills everywhere. Both of us took and released at least fifty trout, taken on the dry fly imitation. In the evening we went down to the Dream Mile (Tobyhanna Creek) and had excellent sport with the Pale Evening Spinner. Lost track of the number of fish taken but we each took home the limit.

May 27—Fished Penns Creek today. Took six nice trout on the Ginger Quill. In the evening while fishing below Pardee, I noticed a beaver swimming across Penns Creek. He was about ninety feet away so decided to try my luck on him. The first cast caught him in the nose and two seconds later I was without a leader. Luckily I pointed my rod directly at him when he became hooked.

May 27—The trout on Spring Creek taking the Black Drake with savage determination. The first cast landed a trout 15 inches, and as it was rather severely hooked, I decided to keep it. Quite a crowd around watching the fun of landing it. About fifty feet farther upstream, I tied into another. By rather strenuous means I turned him away from a clump of submerged brush, and having forgotten my landing net, Lew Kunkel standing nearby, promptly came to my aid. The trout was heavy, in excellent condition, so he was duly knocked on the head to join his companion in the creel. Ten minutes after

Pages from the Diary

starting to fish, I checked out with the limit of two nice trout. "Dutch" Derr, who weighed the fish. kidded me awhile in Pennsylvania Dutch, then subtly turned the conversation to the name of the fly I had taken them on. Sensing the motive. I tried to switch the conversation back into its original channel, but the hints becoming rather broad, I finally succumbed and presented him with the bedraggled Black Drake. And so I left Spring Creek with Dutch's blessing and farewell: "Cum witter Challie. De deutscher mus by en onner steche." ("Come again Charlie. The Dutchmen must stick by each other.")

May 28—Got the biggest thrill of my life today by taking an eighteen inch brown trout that was rising at least ninety feet away. This happened near the big rock at the lower end of the Spring Creek project. Took the trout on a dry fly Ginger Quill. He was rising regularly in a small pocket on the other side of the creek, and I missed him the first time, but on the second cast I succeeded in hooking him firmly. Having forgotten the net, I landed the fish by hand.

May 29—Slipped and fell on a rock today on Penns Creek and broke both my rod and reel. This happened early in the morning and spoiled my sport for the day. Took one 17 inch rainbow trout before the accident occurred.

May 29—Took four brook trout and three large fallfish on Kettle Creek today. Fish taken on a Fan Wing Royal Coachman.

May 29—Alex Sweigart and I fished the North Branch of Middle Creek today. Quite a few flies abroad, but the fishing was poor. Caught a number of Iron Blue Duns that had just emerged from the water. Kept a few alive in a glass jar, but was successful in raising only one of them to maturity. Three days later this fly cast its skin, and the resulting imago was almost an exact duplicate of Ronald's Jenny Spinner. Along Weiker Run, Alex secured for me a few male Brown Drakes, which apparently are the spinners of the Dark Green Drakes found last week in almost the same locality.

May 30—Dad and I fished the North Branch of Middle Creek this evening. A big hatch of Ginger Quills was over the water, but the jinx was on us, for neither of us took a trout.

May 30—Ralph Endriss and I fished the Willowemoc today, but no sooner had we started in than muddy water began coming downstream. Then went down and fished the Beaverkill at the Junction Pool. No luck.

May 30—Ben Baird and I stayed at his hunting camp on Lick Run overnight, then fished the creek till noon. Rather cold, and a few Black Drakes over the water. No trout jumping. Around noon quit fishing and went over to Spring Creek. Saw a few late stragglers of the shad fly hatch which was over the water a few days before. Not many flies in evidence, except some small caddis flies similar to those noticed on Penns Creek a few weeks before. Fish not rising, and poor as usual after the big shad fly hatch.

June 5—Fished the Brodhead—Herman Burgdorf's water—with George Richards, Mel Wood, and Carl Crane. Weather warm and cloudy, ideal for dry fly fishing, but just before the evening rise a heavy rain descended, causing the water to become high and roily. Wood took two trout on a wet fly, the only fish taken by the party. A few Green Drakes over the water. In the evening went down and drank beer at Charlie Rethoret's (Analomink Charlie's) and showed the crowd some colored movies that George and I took while fishing for salmon in New Brunswick.

June 6—Fished Lycoming Creek with Dick Forney (the outdoor writer) today. Took two trout, each about 11 inches long.

June 9—Fished Spring Creek today, Caught three small trout, all of which I returned to the water. Fishing poor, creek cloudy, and weather hot. The Spotted Sedge was over the water in fairly good numbers but failed to interest the trout.

June 11—Ben Baird and I fished Fishing Creek above Mill Hall this evening. No luck. Then went to Lick Run, where we caught five brown trout on bucktails. A few caddis flies over the water but fish were not jumping due to discolored water.

June 13—Fished Hammersleys Forks today. A terrible thunder storm came up and the trees were falling all around me. Took 8 brook trout.

June 18—Fished Sinnemahoning Creek near Huntley and also the Tunnel Hill Pool below. Took two nice trout, one 14 and the other 16 inches long.

June 19—Ed. Schmoke (brother of the well known crippled fly tyer) and I fished the First Fork of the Sinnemahoning today. Where Lushbaugh Creek emptied into the First Fork a thousand or more trout had congregated in the pool to escape the warm water in the big creek. The trout were sick and displayed no interest whatsoever in any kind of flies. Terribly hot.

June 20—While fishing Spring Creek today met my old friend George Phillips the well-known lure manufacturer, who invited me over to fish the Juniata River with him. The big fish were not hitting.

June 26—The fishing being poor on Trout Run, I went down and called on my old angling friends, LaRue Wykoff and Ira Weede. Noticed a rather unusual Mayfly over Kettle Creek this evening. It has clear sparkling wings with a trace of pink at the front edge, a white body, yellowish white legs, and a conspicuous pink egg sack at the end of its abdomen. Sat down and tied up an imitation, on which I took four trout. Could no longer see the fly on account of darkness, so quit fishing. Am going to call the imitation, the White Mayfly. (Note added later) This fly now definitely identified as being *Stenonema rubromaculatum*.

June 28—David Baird and I camped last night along Hammersleys Forks and almost froze. Fished the Forks today, but the stream was high and discolored. The Golden Spinner and the Yellow Sally were both over the water but the trout would not rise. Then tried the quill nymph, on which I took four brook trout. Returned these fish to the water.

June 30—Big hatch of small brown caddis flies over Kettle Creek late this evening. Length of wings about one-fourth of an inch. Trout were taking the fly well, and on an imitation hastily constructed I took ten brook trout. Trout jumping everywhere. Secured a number of the flies and sent them to the caddis fly specialist, H. H. Ross, for identification.

July 1—Ran into an enormous hatch of Yellow Drakes this evening on Middle Creek. The flies came on the water just before dark, and in a short time I took three nice trout on the dry fly. These insects appeared exactly on the same date last year, as well as the year before, only not in such great numbers.

July 3—George Richards and I fished Spring Creek today. Caught six nice trout and kept the two largest. Ran across Clayton Peters, the well-known fly tyer, and in the evening Don Martin furnished us with his account of taking the large 15 pound brown trout on a fly out of Big Spring a short time before. Don won a Field and Stream prize with this fish.

July 4—Spring Creek low and clear today. Extremely hot and no insects over the water except midges. Took eight trout on the small midge pupa fished near the surface using 5X gut. Lost two large trout that broke the leader. Kept two fish, one twelve and the other seventeen inches long.

July 4—Camped last night along Kettle Creek, and fished the Cannonading hole and the Forks today. Took two rainbow trout on the quill nymph, and in the evening took two more on the Yellow Sally. The White Gloved Howdy, the Scorpion Fly, the White Miller, and many green and yellow stone flies were over the water just before dark. Whip-poor-wills whistling everywhere.

July 8—Caught a 16 inch rainbow trout on a stone fly nymph this morning on Spring Creek, and took two smaller fish later on in the evening. Lost an immense trout at the foot of the dam above the Administration building. Midges over the water.

July 10—Spring Creek high and discolored due to recent heavy rains. Managed, however, to take four large trout on a deep running Weezil, fished close to the bottom. This lure exceptionally good in muddy water.

Nov. 28—Received letter today from H. H. Ross, Urbana, Illinois, and feel highly honored over his naming the caddis flies taken on Kettle Creek, June 30th. *Athripsodes wetzeli.*

CHAPTER XV

Fisherman's Weather

WEATHER plays a far more important part in our fishing than the majority of us may realize. That certain fish are more active and bite best under certain weather conditions is well understood by all old-time anglers. Suppose, for instance, we consider various conditions:

HOT WEATHER, CLEAR WATER, BRIGHT SUNSHINE

The fly fisher angling for trout and bass will find such conditions the poorest for his sport. On the other hand, both bait and fly fishermen will find this condition ideal for taking perch, sunfish, crappie, rock bass, fallfish, and pickerel, the latter commonly called pike. This group of fish are lovers of bright sunshine, and are most active at this time. Why this is so is one of the mysteries of nature. It may be that the structure of the eye is such that they can see and find food better at such times; however, whatever the reason, the fact remains that their activity drops off sharply during late evening and after nightfall.

WARM WEATHER, CLEAR WATER, CLOUDY

This is ideal fly fishing weather for both trout and bass, and the cloudier the day, the better the fish will rise to the fly. Mist, however, lying close to the water is not good.

Both trout and bass are easily frightened fish, and it is quite reasonable to presume that cloudy weather, together with an absence of shadows, contributes largely towards making these fish more active, bolder, and less wary in their search for food. It appears also that in this dark cloudy setting, the visibility of the fish is sharpened to an unusual degree. This can be verified by many anglers who may recall incidents when trout rose to the fly on cloudy day from a long way off, and again when they had the faculty of locating quickly the smallest of artificials from great distances.

Another factor which contributes to the great feeding activity of trout and bass in dark surroundings is the unusual presence at such times of uymphs, larvae, etc. on the stream bed. To illustrate: Suppose we pick up a stone on the stream bed and turn it over; any nymphs which may have been clinging to the stone quickly scuttle off to the underside, away from the light; in short, they are afraid of it. In late evening and after dark, however, such nymphs desert their dark hiding places and wander freely about over the stream bed.

I recall one early morning, when after knocking a trout over the head preparatory to putting him in the creel, he disgorged a large number of the white Mayfly nymphs, *Ephemera guttulata,* which burrow in the stream bed. The time of this incident was about one month before the nymph would effect its metamorphosis to the winged fly. Trout of course do not root around at such a depth underneath the stream bed; and the only conclusion to draw was that, under cover of darkness, these nymphs of the Green Drake started wandering about over the stream-bed, and were snapped up by this fish.

I have no doubt at all that trout know how dark the surroundings must be before such underwater life starts roaming around in search of food; and when such activity does start, they in turn begin to prey on the nymphs and larvae. This undoubtedly is the reason why fly fishing is usually good just before nightfall.

From the foregoing one would naturally believe then, that the best time for fly fishing for trout would be in late evenings or after nightfall; however, such is not always the case. Trout rise well to the fly in early morning; and during a long spell of hot, sultry weather, early morning fishing will prove to be the best. The reason for this is that trout, like human beings, are affected by the heat. As evening approaches after a long hot day, the water is still too warm for the trout to display much ambition; however, during the night, the temperature starts falling, and by morning the water has cooled sufficiently for them once again to take an active interest in food.

Warm Weather, Muddy Water, Cloudy

Such weather represents ideal conditions for taking catfish, eels, and trout on worms. These fish quickly realize that the rains—contributing to the muddy water—wash into the streams a great number of angle worms, on which they start feeding. It is perhaps not generally known that many old lunker trout are caught on night crawlers in muddy water immediately following a rain. On mountain streams it is seldom that the water gets really muddy; however, if the water rises and gets slightly murky, then it is in the best condition for taking trout on worms.

Fisherman's Weather

The older I get, the more I am convinced that good fishing hinges directly on light and darkness. I have never taken too much stock in the effect of wind on fishing, particularly the old rhyme:

> When the wind blows from the North,
> The prudent angler goes not forth.
> When the wind blows from the East,
> That's when fishes bite the least.
> When the wind blows from the South,
> It blows the bait in the fish's mouth.
> When the wind blows from the West,
> That's the time fishing is the best.

However I do have faith in some of the old doggerels which prognosticate the weather, such as:

> When the dew is on the grass,
> Rain will never come to pass.
>   and
> Evening red and morning grey,
> Starts the traveler on his way.
> Evening grey, and morning red,
> Brings down showers upon his head.

Some may believe in such predictions, while others don't; however, we must remember that the majority of these prognostications are centuries old, have been handed down from generation to generation, and have weathered the test of time. You be the judge.

APPENDIX

REFERENCE LITERATURE

Alexander, Charles Paul. "The Crane Flies of New York." Part 2, *Biology and Phylogeny*, pp. 695-1042. Cornell University Agriculture Experiment Station, Memoir 38. Ithaca, N.Y., published by the University, June 1920.

American Entomological Society, Transaction of the. Philadelphia, Pa.

Banks, Nathan. *Catalogue of the Neuropteroid Insects* (except Odonata) of the United States. 53 pp. Philadelphia, Pa., American Entomological Society, 1907.

Betten, Cornelius. *The Caddis Flies or Trichoptera of New York State.* N.Y. State Museum Bulletin 292. 576 pp. Albany, N.Y., The University of the State of New York, 1934.

Brues, Charles T. and A. L. Melander. *Classification of Insects.* Bulletin of the Museum of Comparative Zoology at Harvard College. Vol. LXXIII. 672 pp. Cambridge, Mass. Printed for the Museum at Harvard College, 1932.

Canadian Entomologist, The.

Dodds, G. S. "Mayflies from Colorado," pp. 93-114. From *Transactions of the American Entomological Society*, No. 841, issued July 30, 1923.

Felt, Ephraim Porter. *Illustrated Descriptive Catalogue of Some of the More Important and Injurious and Beneficial Insects of New York State.* 52 pp. Bulletin of the New York State Museum No. 37, Vol. 8. Albany, N.Y., University of the State of New York, 1900.

Felt, Ephraim Porter. *A Popular Guide to the Study of Insects.* 147 pp. New York State Museum Handbook No. 6, Albany, N.Y. The University of the State of New York, 1929.

Lutz, Frank E. *Field Book of Insects.* 562 pp. N.Y. & London, G. P. Putnam's Sons, 1918.

Malloch, John R. *The Chironomidae or Midges of Illinois.* pp. 275-543. Bulletin of the Illinois State Laboratory of Natural History, vol. X, Art. VI. Urbana, Ill., 1915.

Metcalf, C. L. *Black Flies and Other Biting Flies of the Adirondacks.* 78 pp. New York State Museum Bulletin No. 289. Albany, N.Y., University of the State of New York, 1932.

Morgan, Ann Haven. *Field Book of Ponds and Streams.* 448 pp. N.Y. & London. G. P. Putnam's Sons, 1930.

Morgan, Ann Haven. "Mayflies of Fall Creek." pp. 93-119. Reprinted from *Annals of the Entomological Society of America*, Vol. IV, No. 2, Columbus, Ohio, 1911.

Needham, J. G. "Burrowing Mayflies of Our Larger Lakes and Streams." Pp. 269-292. From *Bulletin of the Bureau of Fisheries*, Vol. XXXVI, Document No. 883. Washington, D.C., Government Printing Office, July, 1920.

Needham, J. G. and Paul R. Needham. *A Guide to the Study of Fresh Water Biology.* 88 pp. Ithaca, N.Y., Comstock Publishing Co., 1930.

Needham, J. G. and Others. *The Biology of Mayflies.* 759 pp. Ithaca, N.Y., Comstock Publishing Co., 1935.

Needham, J. G. "Aquatic Insects in New York State." Pp. 250-517. *New York State Museum Bulletin 68.* Albany, N. Y., University of the State of New York, 1903.

Needham, J. G. and P. W. Classen. *A Monograph of the Plecoptera or Stone Flies of America North of Mexico.* Pp. 397. Vol. 2, The Thomas Say Foundation of the Entomological Society of America. LaFayette, Ind., 1925.

Needham, J. G. and J. Y. Lloyd. *The Life of Inland Waters.* 438 pp. Ithaca, N.Y., Comstock Publishing Co., 1930.

Ross, H. H. and T. H. Frison. "Studies of Nearctic Aquatic Insects." Pp. 57-99. Vol. 21, Art. 3, Division of the Natural History Survey Division. State of Illinois. Urbana, Ill. Printed by Authority of the State of Illinois, Sept. 1937.

Ross, H. H. *How to Collect and Preserve Insects.* 27 pp. Circular 25 of the State Natural History Survey Division, Urbana, Ill., Feb. 1934.

Ward, Henry Baldwin and George Chandler Whipple. *Fresh Water Biology.* 1111 pp. New York, John Wiley & Sons, 1918.